ELECTRICITY
IN HOUSEHOLDS
AND MICRO-ENTERPRISES

Other titles in this series

Energy Efficiency
Rural Transport
Water Supply

Also published in association with UNIFEM

FOOD CYCLE TECHNOLOGY SOURCE BOOKS

Cereal Processing
Dairy Processing
Drying
Fish Processing
Fruit and Vegetable Processing
Oil Processing
Packaging
Root Crop Processing
Storage
Women's Roles in Technical Innovation

Energy and Environment Technology Source Books

ELECTRICITY
IN HOUSEHOLDS
and MICRO-ENTERPRISES

Joy Clancy

and

Lucy Redeby

INTERMEDIATE TECHNOLOGY PUBLICATIONS
in association with
United Nations Development Fund for Women (UNIFEM) and
Technology and Development Group (TDG), University of Twente,
The Netherlands
2000

Intermediate Technology Publications Ltd,
103–105 Southampton Row, London WC1B 4HL, UK

© The United Nations Development Fund for Women (UNIFEM) 2000
304 East 45th Street, 15th Floor, New York, NY 10017, USA

A CIP record for this book is available from the British Library

ISBN 1 85339 501 3

Typeset by Dorwyn Ltd, Rowlands Castle. Printed in Great Britain by SRP, Exeter

Contents

Acknowledgements

This book represents a collaborative effort between Lucy Redeby of Khalema Redeby and Associates, Lesotho, and Joy Clancy of the Technology and Development Group (TDG), University of Twente in the Netherlands. The authors acknowledge that many people have contributed to the development of the text by making helpful comments to clarify the meaning, by providing case studies and illustrations and by giving moral support and encouragement. Their help is much appreciated.

Lucy Redeby was based for three months at TOOLConsult in the Netherlands, where she prepared the first draft in collaboration with Joy Clancy and Margaret Skutsch from TDG. During that period, Elizabeth Muguti from Zimbabwe was simultaneously working with Saskia Everts on a companion source book, and they, despite their own tight schedule, also found time to assist Lucy. Joy, Margaret and Alfred Stobbelar (from TDG) prepared a first manuscript for circulation to test readers' reactions. The comments by Ruth Lechte (ECOWOMAN, Fiji), Stephen Vardigans (Independent Training Consultant), Ton de Wilde (Independent Consultant) and Eric Hyman (ATI, Washington) resulted in a revision of the text by Joy. Ruth and Stephen provided case studies and made valuable contributions to the checklists and training parts of Chapter 7. Lucy Redeby, Christina Aristanti (ARECOP, Indonesia), Tobias Chipare (ITDG Zimbabwe), Saskia Everts, Margaret Skutsch (who helped us not to become too technical), Giles Stacey (Wind Energy Consultant, Englishworks, the Netherlands) and Margaret Karsens (ETC, Leusden, The Netherlands) acted as a second panel of test readers. Their comments enabled Joy to finalize the manuscript.

Throughout the preparation of the book, Marilyn Carr and Lis Joosten of UNIFEM provided comments, support and encouragement which helped us complete the work.

The funding for this source book was made available by UNIFEM with a cost-sharing contribution from the Government of Sweden.

Joy Clancy, July 2000

1
The benefits of electricity

Introduction

MANY PEOPLE IN remote areas of the world still have no access to electricity. The World Bank estimated that in 1990, 820 million people in rural areas had no access to grid electricity, which is around 15.5% of the world's population. Extension of the grid in rural areas is slow because of the high capital costs involved and utilities are finding it hard to raise the necessary funds. Other people live in areas which are already electrified but cannot afford the connection fee and cost of wiring. Often the quality of the supply is poor and unreliable.

Most people would like electricity in their home or in their workplace, particularly for lighting. The benefits are immediately obvious: it is much safer than candles or kerosene lanterns; it is more convenient, cleaner and gives a better quality light. Electricity can also be used to power radios, refrigerators, drills and computers, as well as cooking stoves and microwave ovens. Such appliances are part of modern life and are in demand wherever electricity is available.

In general, using electricity saves time, can contribute to improvements in health and can save money compared with other energy sources. Electricity is valued because it is a very convenient (it makes life a little easier), clean and modern type of energy. It is instantly controllable at the point of use; an electric device can be operated merely by flicking a switch. However, for many people these benefits may seem unattainable either because of the non-availability of the facility or lack of funds.

Obtaining electricity from the grid is only one of several possible options. There are various ways of generating electricity which are suitable for use by rural and remote communities or by individual (urban and non-urban) householders. This book introduces some of the other possibilities for having access to electricity independent of the national grid. People in developing countries are already using electricity generated by stand-alone (that is not linked to the main grid) technologies, such as diesel generators, micro-hydro, windmills, solar (photovoltaic) panels, gasifiers, biogas generators, steam engines and batteries. These stand-alone systems frequently represent a more environmentally friendly means of generating electricity than large power stations feeding into the national grid. This source book explains how these technologies work and under what conditions. It can be used to help in identifying suitable technologies for producing electricity in the quantities used by households, micro-enterprises and small communities in a particular location.

Some stand-alone systems do not permit the use of all the equipment and tools that can be used with grid-generated electricity. Some equipment is too expensive to run, for example high-powered thermal devices such as stoves and water heaters, and some types of equipment are sensitive to the quality of the electricity produced, for example standard micro-computers and microwave cookers. When considering access to electricity and its benefits, it is important to be aware of these limitations and to compare the electrical and non-electrical options to avoid building up unrealistic expectations.

Using this book

The book is designed for people with little technical background or previous knowledge of electricity and the technologies used to generate it. The aim is to raise awareness of the capabilities of these technologies and to help in making informed decisions about the different options.

A valid question might be: why a special source book on electricity for *women*? Surely everyone benefits from access to an electricity supply, not just women? Of course, this is true; there are benefits to households, to small businesses and to the community as a whole when a village is electrified (see Box 1.1). However, there are a number of reasons why women in particular stand to gain from having access to electricity. Generally, women spend a lot of time in the house and are involved in daily housekeeping tasks such as preparing food, cooking and cleaning. Electricity for lighting, cooking, and running household appliances can make a significant difference to the amount of time housework takes, as well as reducing drudgery. Women are also concerned about the education of their children and recognize the benefits that a few hours of study in the evenings can bring. The high quality of electric light puts less strain on the eyes when reading and writing.

Women are increasingly becoming involved in productive activities either based in the house or in a workshop or commercial premises. These activities generate income which help to maintain the household, and help women to become independent financially. Micro-enterprises in which women are often involved include: hair salons, knitting and sewing businesses, bakeries, food processing, cafés, vegetable and fruit canning, bottling of drinks, grain milling, dairies, tin smithies, repair shops, handicrafts, cooling drinks and chilled water production. It is clear that these enterprises use energy, often biomass fuels such as firewood, charcoal or kerosene, for example. The replacement of these sources of energy by electricity could result in a more comfortable and healthier working environment, greater efficiency and higher profits – if for no other reason than lighting in the evening permits extended working hours. The use of electricity may also allow the small business to develop in ways that are not possible without it. A small hair salon can modernize by adopting electric hairdryers; a drinks stall can refrigerate its drinks to make them more refreshing; a tailoring shop can improve productivity by using electric machines; battery-charging stations can be opened. Should the business grow in size the entrepreneur may consider using a computer for the accounts and paperwork – something quite impossible without electricity. This also opens up new business opportunities selling telecommunications services, such as faxes and telephone calls, to the local community.

Many countries are now changing their laws to allow the private generation and sale of electricity, which presents exciting new opportunities for women to become energy entrepreneurs. Unfortunately, electricity is often regarded as 'men's business' and women dealing with technical issues in companies and non-governmental organizations (NGOs) working in this area are very much in the minority. We hope this book will be a catalyst in changing this situation!

Box 1.1: Benefits of using electricity

Households

Allows utilization of labour-saving small household electrical appliances: irons, blenders, kettles, refrigerators, washing machines and fans.

Lighting at night means that productive activities can continue beyond the period of daylight.

Cleaner and better quality lighting.

As a cooking source.

Entertainment, e.g. radios, TV.

Micro-Enterprises

Enables the use of special appliances such as hairdryers, blenders and computers.

Provides lighting for better working conditions.

Provides cooling/heating for better working conditions.

Access to modern office equipment and communications systems, e.g. fax, computers, the Internet, telephones.

Communities

Makes street lighting possible, thus increasing safety and security.

Refrigeration of vaccines and other medicines in clinics and hospitals, leading to overall improvements in health.

Refrigeration of local agricultural produce, such as meat, fish, dairy and poultry products, can lead to improved nutrition.

Better prices for products due to better food preservation.

Prolongs hours for reading and studying in the evening and at night.

Increases possibilities for getting employment.

Increases quality of life generally, which may lead to reduced urban migration.

Access to communications systems, e.g. fax, computers, telephones, enabling contact with relatives living and working elsewhere.

The book is therefore intended to provide resource material for use by extension workers, trainers and project staff working with women, particularly in rural areas, who consider that access to electricity can play a significant role in their projects. Women's groups, active in promoting women's enterprises and education, may wish to use it for self-study or discussion. The book provides only an introduction to the subject. For more detailed information the reference books, Internet sites and organizations listed at the end may be consulted. Local organizations, such as Ministries of Energy, universities and NGOs are often useful sources of information.

Scope of the source book

This book is concerned with the small-scale generation of electricity for a limited number of users. This could mean a single family, for their home use, or for a small family business such as many women operate from home. This is often called a 'micro-enterprise', which in this book is defined as a small-scale, private, income-generating activity, employing not more than five people.

The electricity consumption for these kinds of initiatives is generally estimated at between 10 and 20 kilowatt-hours

---

Case study: Solar power provides income generation in Ghana

Margaret Anane lives at Asuhyiae in the Teppa Region of Ashanti in Ghana. She is in her early 40s. Her husband is in his sixties. They have seven children, four boys and three girls. They own a cocoa farm at Sefwi in the Western Region which is managed by hired hands as a result of the old age of her husband. Margaret visits the cocoa farm twice a year during the harvest season.

Margaret has another farm at Asuhyiae where the family lives. They cultivate mainly plantain and yams. Margaret's house is directly opposite the Solar Service Centre. The Centre was established by a CIDA Project and has been equipped with solar lights, TV and radio, and also sells battery charging services to the residents of Asuhyiae and the surrounding villages. Before the Solar Centre was installed, batteries were transported to Teppa for charging on the main grid.

As a result of the solar lighting and TV, the area in front of Margaret's house and the Centre had become very busy and lively in the evening and a flourishing night market had emerged. Margaret had become totally convinced of the reliability of the solar lighting system and the opportunity to use the lights for business purposes. She approached the attendants at the Centre about acquiring her own lighting system. She travelled to The University of Science and Technology in Kumasi, about 60 miles from the village, to discuss her plans with the Director of the CIDA Project. Margaret went back to organize the funds to buy a system and nearly six months later, soon after the cocoa harvest, she returned to Kumasi to make the down-payment of 2 million cedis, approximately US$900. She was also advised to purchase a kerosene refrigerator, since the solar fridge is far more expensive.

Margaret is now the proud owner of a $100W_p$ solar-powered system, which is able to run lighting, a TV and a radio. What is more remarkable is that she has renovated one room in the house and converted it into a popular shopping and entertainment spot. The people of Asuhyiae are farmers and mainly cultivate tomatoes. The shop is usually closed during the day when Margaret also visits her farm, but is open from 6pm until midnight.

The full cost of the system is 3.8 million cedis. With 2 million down payment, the rest will be paid up in two years, in two instalments, each one at the end of the cocoa season.

With the current power rationing throughout the country, Margaret's business is really on the upswing, especially on days when the lights are off at Teppa, the district capital. Margaret has now opened up a battery-charging business based on photovoltaics, bringing yet another development to her community.

Source: Prof F. Akuffo, University of Science and Technology, Kumasi, Ghana

---

(kWh) over a 24-hour period. This is enough energy for a household or micro-enterprise to: cook on a stove for 2 hours, light three light bulbs for 10 hours, keep a refrigerator and fan on continuously, do a 10-minute job with a drilling machine, work with a computer for 2 hours and use a kettle to boil water for half an hour. This book focuses on the technologies which produce electricity in amounts likely to be used by individual households, micro-enterprises or small communities:

○ Diesel generators
○ Micro-hydro
○ Wind energy
○ Solar and photovoltaic (PV) energy
○ Gasifiers
○ Biogas
○ Steam
○ Batteries (as a support to the other technologies).

It is rare that electricity will be used for all activities within the household and micro-enterprise. The question is: when is electricity the most appropriate energy form? The main considerations are the end-use (electricity is not the most efficient way of providing space heating, for example), costs (both of buying the equipment and running it) and benefits in each case. Of course, the use of electricity can increase in stages as resources allow, starting with a few electric lights and gradually expanding through the acquisition of different appliances. Some electricity-generating technologies allow for this gradual expansion. Others, however, are of a fixed size (production capacity), which means that a careful plan needs to be made for the amount of power needed both at present and in the future. It is also possible to combine different electricity-generating options. These are known as hybrid systems. An obvious example is batteries combined with other stand-alone technologies, for example solar and wind electricity, to act as insurance when the resource is temporarily not available, on cloudy or wind-less days. It is also possible to use PV and diesel, wind and PV, as well as PV, wind and diesel.

This book discusses various possibilities based on resources that may be available in rural areas for generating electricity independently of the national grid. Descriptions of the technologies and their costs are given, as well as their different requirements in terms of inputs and skill needed for installation and operation. Some straightforward information and advice is given on using electricity; indications on how to calculate the size of technology needed; and how to choose appropriate appliances. It also outlines the simple precautions that need to be taken to use electricity safely to avoid accidents or fire.

The book is intended as a starting point for obtaining a basic understanding of the technologies, to give women the confidence to discuss with experts what the possibilities are for themselves, their households, their businesses and their communities. The book is not prescriptive, since costings are site specific and prices change rapidly. For detailed sizing and costings more expert advice will be needed.

Case studies from developing countries, highlighting successful women's initiatives with the technologies can be found throughout the text.

Anyone reading the book should find answers to the following types of questions which are of direct relevance to women thinking about electricity for use in their household or existing or planned micro-enterprises:

○ How much electricity would the household or the micro-enterprise use per month?
○ How does the national grid work?
○ What alternatives are there to grid electricity?
○ What are the advantages and disadvantages of the different stand-alone electricity generation systems?
○ Which systems are suited for individual households and which for a mini-grid capable of meeting the electricity demands of a small community?

○ Are there particular problems or implications women might face with the technology?
○ Is electricity safe to use and what precautions need to be taken to ensure that it is safe?

Chapter 2 considers factors to be taken into account when making any decision related to obtaining electricity supply. It starts by clarifying some of the terms commonly used when talking about electricity, and goes on to cover a number of important issues such as how to assess the amount of electricity likely to be used and the time of day at which it is needed.

Chapter 3 discusses electricity from the national grid. It explains how a grid works and how to find out what the possibility, and the costs, would be for joining the grid, both for the individual and for the small community. Some suggestions are made on how to lobby for extension of the grid to a community.

Chapter 4 describes eight different stand-alone electricity-generating systems

providing information about how much power they produce, indications of costs, what resources are needed to ensure reliable operation and environmental impacts. A summary of the different options is made which allows for comparisons to be made.

Chapter 5 outlines a simple financial appraisal method such as might be undertaken by households or micro-enterprises.

Chapter 6 looks at wiring in the household and micro-enterprise and safety issues.

Chapter 7 provides a checklist to help in the evaluation of the options, as well as providing ideas on how to support women's initiatives to gain access to electricity.

Chapter 8 lists resources (books, the Internet and organizations) where information about the generation and use of electricity can be found.

The Appendix takes a slightly more technical look at electricity and explains some of the terms in more detail. The book can be read and understood without reading this section.

2
Getting connected

Introduction: Making a preliminary assessment

WHEN THE GRID arrives in a village or community, who gets access is determined by how much it will cost to be connected and how much it will cost to use the electricity. If grid connection is likely to be at some far distant date in the future, the alternative to doing without is to consider investing in stand-alone generating systems either individually, as a group or as a whole community. A stand-alone system is sometimes called a remote power system (RPS) which is the term used throughout this book[1]. RPS include diesel engines and systems based on renewable energy resources. Cost is a major determinant in selecting an appropriate RPS: comparison should always be made with diesel engines since this is a mature, widely available technology with an extensive existing maintenance and spare parts infrastructure, and available in a range of sizes which makes it easy to match both existing and future demand. Not all RPS are so flexible or easily maintained.

Although making a preliminary assessment of grid connection or an RPS does not require detailed technical knowledge, to accurately cost and determine the size of an RPS does need expert help, for example, from universities or NGOs. The power company (also known as the utility) may be prepared to assist, since they sometimes use stand-alone systems as an interim strategy to introduce consumers to the uses of electricity and to create suffi-

cient demand to ensure that grid extension is cost effective.

Assessing the acceptability of the cost of electricity, whether from the grid or an RPS, can be broken down into a number of steps:

○ Identifying who needs energy and for what purpose
○ Assessing whether or not electricity is the most appropriate energy form for meeting needs
○ Calculating how much electricity is needed
○ Assessing the costs of electricity from the options available.

An initial assessment of electricity supply options can be made with the help of this book. This chapter begins with an explanation of some of the common terms and concepts encountered in the world of electricity generation. An understanding of the terms commonly used by professionals is helpful in determining what electricity can do. It will also give potential consumers more confidence in dealing with utility staff and other experts when discussing the options. The second part of the chapter discusses how to assess needs and calculate demand.

Electrical terminology

This section explains some of the common terms that are used by electricity

---

[1] Other terms include independent power producer (IPP) or independent rural power producer (IRPP).

Box 2.1: Common electrical terms

Electricity is essentially a flow of electrons (particles or packets of electrical energy so small that they are not visible to the human eye) carrying energy known as an electric current along a wire. The generation of an electric current enables the operation of electrical equipment, such as radios and lights.

Volt = A unit of measurement of voltage (V). Voltage can be thought of as the force which pushes electricity along wires, similar to the pressure which forces water through a pipe.

The two most common voltages used in electric circuits from grid electricity within households are 110V and 220V. However, in some countries 120V or 240V are used. Batteries also produce electric currents but use lower voltages (for example, dry cell batteries can range from 1.3 to 9V, while car batteries come in 12, 24 and 48V versions).

Current is the rate of flow of electrons (hence electrical energy) through a circuit. The unit of measurement of current is the amp (A).

Batteries are commonly described in terms of the amount of current they can supply per hour, using a unit of measurement the *Ampere hour* sometimes written as amp-hour (Ah). The total amount of energy stored in a battery is also given in Ah.

1Ah = 1 amp-hour, that is a current of 1A flowing for 1 hour.

Energy is the ability to do work. Energy comes in different forms, chemical energy when burning wood, kinetic energy when the wind blows, and electrical energy to operate a TV.

Energy is measured in joules (J). A joule is a very small quantity of energy and so the quantities of energy used to do many ordinary tasks are measured in kilojoules (kJ, where 1kJ= 1000J) or megajoules (MJ, where 1MJ = 1 000 000J).

Electrical energy is more usually expressed in Watt hours (Wh) which is also a small amount of energy. Electricity bills are usually expressed in kilowatt hours (kWh, where 1kWh = 1000Wh).

It is possible to convert kWh to MJ and MJ to kWh using the relationship:
1kWh = 3.6MJ

Power is the rate at which energy is supplied or used. This statement can be written in the form of a simple equation:

$$\text{Power} = \frac{\text{energy}}{\text{time}}$$

This relationship tells us that energy can be supplied or consumed at different rates. The amount of energy needed to boil a litre of water is constant when the intitial temperature of the water is the same. However, if the water is needed at boiling point in 2 minutes, it will require more power than if the boiling point is reached in 10 minutes.

Power is usually measured in watts.

Watt (W) = A measurement of power, that is the amount of energy consumed or generated per unit of time. 1W = 1 Joule/sec, which is a very small amount of power.

Appliances which use electricity are sold in terms of their power rating. Light bulbs are sold at 40W, 60W and 100W; fluorescent tubes are typically 40W.

A 100W light bulb uses more energy per minute (or any other time period) than a 60W bulb. A 40W bulb uses less energy, in the same time period, than a 60W bulb.

Electricity-generating equipment is also described in terms of the amount of power it can deliver. For example, 20MW is the size of a power station, which means it can generate 20 million J of electricity per second. This is sufficient electricity for a town.

Kilowatt (kW) 1kW = 1000 W, for example 25×40W bulbs would need 1kW.

Megawatt (MW) = 1 000 000 Watts = the size of a small power station.

Kilowatt-hour (kWh) = The amount of energy consumed when operating equipment rated at one kilowatt for one hour.

Box 2.2: Choice of current for non-grid generation and its influence on costs

Grid electricity and most stand-alone systems convert one form of energy into mechanical energy by turning a shaft which is coupled to a generator. The generator converts the mechanical energy into electrical energy. The electrical current produced can have two different forms: alternating or direct.

Alternating Current (AC) = an electric current that reverses or alternates its direction at regular intervals. The rate or frequency with which the current alternates varies, although most conventional grid supplies use 50 or 60 Hertz.

AC is the type of current supplied by utilities through the grid to households and micro-enterprises. Most common household equipment operates on this form of electricity. The electrical generator which produces AC is an alternator.

Direct Current (DC) = an electric current that flows in only one direction through the circuit. This is the type of electricity supplied by batteries and photovoltaic panels. The electrical generator which produces DC is a dynamo.

AC can be converted to DC with a rectifier and likewise DC can be converted to AC by means of an inverter. This is not technically difficult. However, there are costs both for the inverter itself and there are always some losses associated with the conversion process (5 – 10%). Inverters can also be noisy. Equipment designed for AC cannot run directly on DC, it needs an inverter. The same applies to equipment designed for DC. For example, charging a car battery from the mains grid supply requires a rectifier.

The utility can produce either AC or DC electricity. However, it chooses to supply AC for bulk transmission. This is because the voltage of AC can be easily and at reasonable cost increased or decreased by transformers. Bulk supplies of electricity are transmitted at high voltages (because the losses are lower, which keeps costs down). However, before the electricity is supplied to the consumer the voltage is reduced (stepped-down) to much lower values for safety reasons.

(Continued over)

Households or micro-enterprises which intend to generate their own electricity from stand-alone systems, particularly from PV, batteries and small wind systems, have to give careful thought to which type of electricity they are going to produce. AC has a number of advantages related to the costs. Due to the fact that grid electricity uses AC, most appliances and equipment used in the electricity circuit, such as generators, switches, and circuit breakers, utilize AC which allows for economies of scale to be built into the prices of equipment. Equipment suitable for households and micro-enterprises is also available for DC but is correspondingly more expensive than the AC equivalent; however, the extra cost can be offset by not having to purchase and run an inverter. Some equipment, for example an electric clock, requires AC of a specific frequency for correct operation. DC appliances are usually designed for 12 or 24V (and occasionally 36V) operation. They are generally more efficient than their AC equivalents. On the other hand there is less choice available at present and replacements may also be difficult to find. This can be expected to change as the use of stand-alone systems based on renewable energy sources increases. Buildings might already have been wired for AC.

In general, if the power demand is less than a few of hundred watts and the distance from RPS to appliance is not too far, (as, for example, one might expect in a solar PV household system), a 12V DC supply would generally be sufficient. A higher power demand and longer cables would require a 24V DC supply. If power demand is greater than 1.5kW and/or the transmission distance is long, for example as might be expected with a community micro-hydro system, then an AC system is more appropriate.

planners and professionals (Box 2.1). A detailed understanding of the scientific concepts of electricity is not necessary to make an assessment of the options nor is it needed to use electricity. However, those readers who would like to understand a little more about the way electricity works should consult the Appendix.

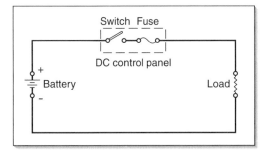

Figure 2.1: A simple electric circuit

Assessing electricity needs

An assessment of needs is relatively easy for an individual home or micro-enterprise. However, for a community it is a more complex process, since there are different groups involved, each with their own needs and access to resources. There are three basic steps in assessing electricity requirements and people's willingness to pay:

○ Who needs energy for what?
○ Prioritizing needs
○ How much electricity is needed?

What is the energy needed for? Although people are more interested in the activity the energy is needed for rather than the energy itself, they may require some help in identifying their needs, since they may not be familiar with the possibilities of using electricity other than for lighting. In Nepal, local electricity user organizations have been established with the help of local community motivators, both men and women, to stimulate the use of electricity. A long list of needs might emerge and it is quite possible that women will not be able to pay for all of these. They will need to decide on priorities, for which they need to be aware of the costs. Gender differences within households have also to be taken into account when assessing needs and priorities. For example, women may favour lights in the kitchen whereas men may prefer an external security light to discourage thieves. Seasonal variations in demand also need to be taken into account. Are the expectations realistic? Does a community consider lighting in a school a priority over desks?

There are costs involved not only with obtaining the supply and using it, but also in buying the appliances. How much can a household afford to pay? Would rechargeable batteries rather than a direct grid connection be acceptable?

Stimulating income-generating activities is important to the community for many reasons. The potential for such activities can induce the electricity utility to bring a supply to the community if it can be demonstrated that there will be larger users than households with a corresponding ability to pay. For a community electricity generating scheme, entrepreneurs using electricity during the day will help pay the investment and operating costs for the system and will ensure that maximum use is made of it. Women entrepreneurs will need advice on new business opportunities that can arise from an electricity supply – e.g. dairy, grain-mill, communications centre (fax, telephone, computers). Irrespective of whether it is grid or RPS, they will need to assess how much and what type of energy they will use and when it is required (on a seasonal and daily basis). What is the market for their product? How secure is it? What can they afford to pay for the electricity? Would a bank lend them the start-up finance?

People also need to be aware of the limitations of the different electricity supply options. Grid extension should present no problem in meeting the usually modest demands of households and micro-enterprises. However, some of the RPS can only meet small demands at reasonable costs and can suffer from supply disruption due to energy resource availability (for example, a shortage of diesel or lack of sunshine or wind) (see Chapter 4). These disruptions can be overcome with back-ups and storage, which add to the costs. Grid electricity makes very little demand on the consumer but RPS place regular demands on the owner for maintenance. Whilst these tasks are usually neither arduous nor time-consuming in themselves, owners need to be aware of what is involved and the consequences of not carrying out the tasks. They also need training, so that they are confident of being able to undertake the tasks themselves.

Financial constraints may mean that all energy demands cannot be met. Therefore some form of prioritization has to be made and some end-uses will have to wait until the future when incomes are sufficient or other forms of energy can be used. In helping to assign priorities the question can be asked: Is electricity the most appropriate form of energy for this particular activity? It is possible to classify electricity needs into three categories:

○ *necessary* – those uses for which electricity is entirely or almost essential, e.g. lighting, electronics equipment

Table 2.1: Power ratings of electrical equipment

Appliance	Power rating (W)	Sample power consumption on a daily basis[a] (kWh/day)
Lighting options		
Light bulb	25, 40, 60, 75, 100	0.75
Fluorescent light	4–8, 18–36–58, 75	0.2
Security light	100–200	1
Household equipment		
Space heater (multiple bars/rods)	2000	12
Single bar/rod space heater	1200	7.2
Cassette player	20–60	0.2
Freezer	800	3.6
Refrigerator (rating depends on volume)	100–300	1.5
2-ring cooker	2000	4
Stove (rings plus oven)	5000–12000	2.5
Rice cooker	1000	0.75
Microwave cooker	500–1500	0.5
Food mixer/blender	80–200	0.03
Kettle	1000–2000	0.5
Hot water cylinder	1000–3000	10
Iron	450–1000	0.09
Radio	5–30	0.09
Black and white television	20–75	0.03
Colour television	40–200	0.2
Video	10–40	0.02
Mosquito repellent	5	0.06
Shaver	60	0.003
Micro-enterprise/community equipment		
Sewing machine	80	3
Photocopier	400	1
Computer	100–200	1.6
Printer Dot matrix Laser	30–50 600–900	0.05 1.6
Fax machine	40	0.96
Overhead projector	300	1.2
Ceiling fan	60–100	0.4
Air conditioner	750–1500	7
Electric drill	300	0.15
Hand-held hairdryer	600–1500	0.01
Cash register	10–30	0.25

Note a: These figures are indicative only and actually depend upon the time assumed for operation of the appliance
Sources: Congress of the United States Office of Technology Assessment (1992); Gujerat Energy Agency; ERDC

Example 2.1: Household electricity demand

A household with three 60W filament light bulbs, a radio and a refrigerator needs the following amount of electrical energy:

10 hours of lighting	$3 \times 60W \times 10h$	$= 1800Wh$
3 hours of radio listening	$1 \times 30W \times 3h$	$= 90Wh$
24 hours of refrigerator use	$1 \times 100W \times 24h \times 0.5$	$= 1200Wh$

(The refrigerator motor runs intermittently so it is assumed that it is only using electricity for half of the time)

Total amount of energy   3090Wh

In this case the household would need a system capable of delivering at least 3090Wh a day (or 3.09kWh/day).

○ *convenient* – uses for which substitutes are adequate but lack the convenience, control or cleanliness of electricity, e.g. food storage, air conditioning, pumping
○ *non-essential* – uses for which other forms of energy can easily, and in most cases more efficiently, perform the same function, e.g. low temperature space- or water-heating

These categories can help people to judge priorities. They also need to know the costs of operating appliances. These costs should be made on the basis of the different generating electricity options and also on other appropriate energy forms, e.g. lighting from grid, solar home system and kerosene. Table 2.1 gives some representative figures for electrical energy consumption in some common pieces of equipment.

How much electricity is needed?

To answer the question how much electricity is needed, the appliances to be used, how much energy they consume and an estimate of how long they will be in use daily, need to be known. Table 2.1 gives an overview of the power ratings of some typical electrical equipment used in households and micro-enterprises. Examples of calculating demand assessment are shown in Examples 2.1 (household), 2.2 (micro-enterprise) and 2.3 (community). As mentioned, it is sometimes possible to start with a few appliances and gradually acquire more. For example, one could start with using just one or two light bulbs. When choosing an electricity generating technology, it is important to remember that electricity consumption is likely to increase in the future. The technology chosen will have to satisfy not only present needs, but also increases in demand as incomes grow in the future. On the other hand it is important not to overestimate demand, because under-used capacity is an expensive waste of investment.

Community or individual electricity system?

If a grid is present, then it is an individual household's or micro-enterprise's decision to apply for a connection. If there is no grid, the community may decide to join together to lobby the power utility to bring the grid to the community. Some aspects of how to organize this are given in more detail in Chapter 3.

If the community is in a remote area, where the terrain is difficult, the prospect of the grid reaching the community lies in the distant future, if at all. The community may then decide to join together to purchase an individual (stand-alone) system to establish a local micro- or mini-grid with a centralized generating system. This has the benefit of sharing costs and operation and maintenance requirements. However, community-run systems bring other challenges associated with the management of the system. The community as a whole has to decide how much electricity will be supplied to each individual household; who is responsible for the collection of fees and the operation, maintenance and repair of the system. Many communities do not have experience of the type of communal organization and management required to operate and maintain a technical system. Women may be able to play a leading role in the management to ensure that their needs are taken into account (see Chapter 7). Attention will need to be paid to women acquiring the appropriate skills to prevent them from being marginalized in the committees.

The management structure will need to enjoy the support and confidence of the whole community since it will be responsible for community money. The management may also have to make difficult decisions when consumers have not paid their bills. This can be problematical when dealing with relatives and friends. The legal system may not be adequate for dealing with these issues.

Social and economic aspects of the system also need to be considered. What will be the effect on the community if only wealthy people gain access to the electricity? Are there any ways in which the poorer members of the community can benefit? – for example, lighting for the community or religious centre? On the other hand, a well thought out and planned system can bring advantages in strengthening the community and bringing it closer together. There will also be a small number of jobs created for running and maintaining the system.

Before choosing the technical and management systems, it is useful to do some research into how other communities have dealt with these issues, preferably visiting schemes to see what lessons have been learnt. It is important to contact the power company, even if considering an isolated grid, to discuss their future plans for extending the national grid. There are, unfortunately, many examples of villages that have established community grids, only to find that within a few months the utility brings the national grid line to the community.

Example 2.2: Electricity demand in a micro-enterprise

A women's co-operative sets up a sewing micro-enterprise. There are three rooms: a work area, an office and a kitchen where the women take their breaks and cook. The women make an inventory of the equipment they would like to have in their work place. The list consists of three sewing machines, two fans and five filament light bulbs (three in the work room and one each in the office and kitchen). The office should have a photocopier, fax, computer and laser printer. In the kitchen they propose a 2-ring cooker, a refrigerator, a kettle and a hot water cylinder. The working day for the enterprise is 8 hours for 250 days a year. They calculate their potential power demand and energy use as follows:

(Continued over)

	Equipment	Power demand (W)	Time in use in hours	Daily energy use (Wh)
Work room	3 Sewing machines	80	6	1440
	2 Fans	60	8	960
	5 Filament lamp bulbs	75	8	3000
Office	Photocopier	50 (stand-by)	7	350
		750 (working)	1	750
	Fax	40	24	960
	Computer	200	8	1600
	Laser printer	600	1	600
Kitchen	Kettle	1500	0.5	300
	Refrigerator	300	24*	1500
	2-ring cooker	2000	1	2000
	Hot water cylinder	3000	2	6000

although motor runs intermittantly

The maximum power demand of the enterprise is 9125W (9.1kW) and the daily energy use is around 19460Wh (approximately 20kWh). The actual daily total will vary, depending on how much of the time equipment in intermittent use, such as the laser printer, is used. On an annual basis, the enterprise is using around 5000kWh of electricity.

The women can use these figures to estimate their electricity bill from the grid (national or local community mini-grid) or the running costs of an RPS. The figures can also help them to make a number of other choices. If they use 40W fluorescent tube lights instead of the filament lamps (which would not reduce their lighting quality), they would need 175W less power and save 1400Wh per day (350kWh a year; approximately 7%). Their calculations also identify two major uses of power in the micro-enterprise; the hot water heater and the cooker. These are non-productive uses of the electricity. The women therefore might like to consider whether there are cheaper alternatives, for example, solar water heaters for the hot water and efficient wood stoves for cooking. (Costs would not be the only criteria on which the decisions would be made – see Chapters 5 and 7.) Not using electricity for cooking and water heating would reduce the power demand by 5kW and reduce electricity use by 1760kWh/year (35%). This potentially offers significant savings on investment costs and running costs, although it would need to be compared with the alternatives.

The women could consider selling office services to other community members (fax, photocopying) which would help them to repay investment costs.

Example 2.3: Community electricity

A small community has ten houses. Each house has two 18W fluorescent light bulbs and a radio with a power rating of 30W. The average use of the light bulbs is 4 hours a day, so each house needs about 144Wh per day for lighting. The average use of the radio is 3 hours a day, which means 90Wh per day for listening to the radio. The average use of electrical energy per house is 234Wh per day. For the community as a whole this means a total consumption of electrical energy of 2340Wh or 2.3kWh per day. If the community wants to have one centralized system for the supply of electricity, this system should be capable of producing at least 2.3kWh a day. This is known as the system capacity. For technical reasons, the system capacity should exceed the maximum demand by about 15%.

The system would meet only present needs and it is quite likely that demand would increase as people become more aware of the possibilities for using electricity and their incomes rise. The size of the system has to be optimized so that it is not too large and the generating equipment is running at low loads, therefore operating inefficiently and wasting money, but it is large enough to meet future increases in demand. This type of system sizing needs expert advice. If possible, a modular system should be selected, which can be easily added to as demand grows. In addition, the system would be in use only at night, and therefore consideration could be given to see if a productive enterprise, such as a grain-mill, could be running during the day to help offset the investment costs.

3
Electricity from the grid

THE GRID HAS a number of advantages for the end-user, such as convenience. When considering investing in stand-alone electricity systems it is always useful to compare these options with the grid, in terms of the costs involved and other factors.

How the grid works

The national grid is a network of electricity lines, underground cables, wires, substations and transformers running from the power station, to transmit and distribute electricity to consumers in cities, towns and rural areas, in order to meet the demand at any time (see Figure 3.1a). This central production of electricity exists in almost all countries, although access, particularly in areas outside the cities and major towns is severely restricted. It has been estimated that presently around 70% of the people in the developing world remain without access to grid electricity.

Grid electricity supply is the responsibility of a public or private power company or utility. The activities involved in supplying electricity through a grid can be divided into three components:

○ **Generation** involves the production of electricity by the conversion of another energy form. Generation takes place in central power stations with capacities in the megawatt range (although some older power stations may be capable of generating only kilowatts). Power stations can be thermal (oil, gas or coal-fired), hydro (which uses the energy in water stored in dams), or nuclear. Nowadays more environmentally friendly systems based on renewable energy sources are appearing; for example, in Europe, the USA, Australia and New Zealand, there are several large-scale commercial wind systems feeding into national grids.

○ **Transmission**. Following generation, electricity goes through transformers which increase the voltage (usually from 25 000V) to a level considered appropriate for transporting or transmitting the electricity (up to 400 000V). High voltages are used because the losses will be lower.

○ **Distribution**. Electricity is taken from the national grid at substations and reduced first to 132 000V and then to lower voltages for distribution to different parts of a country; the supply is reduced to 33 000V for large industrial consumers. The supply is further reduced to 11 000V for distribution to towns, villages and to small industrial consumers (see figure 3.2). The voltage is finally reduced by transformers to 415, 240, 220 and 110V for supply to individual customers. (This last step is known as reticulation.) In Europe, Africa and most parts of Asia 220V is the usual standard, whereas in the Americas it is 110V.

One company may be responsible for all three components of the grid, or a number of companies may share the tasks.

Organizational structure of grid supply

The organization of the electricity supply varies between countries (see Box 3.1). In the past the generation and distribution of electricity has been controlled at a

Figure 3.1a: The national grid

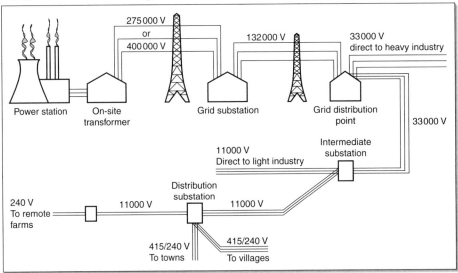

Figure 3.1b: A mini-grid illustrating the integration of different energy conversion technologies

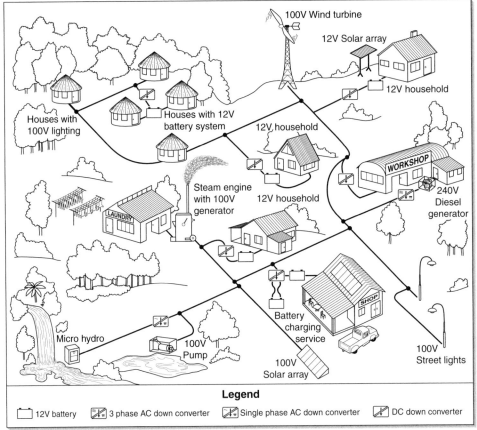

Figure 3.2: Transformers in a grid system

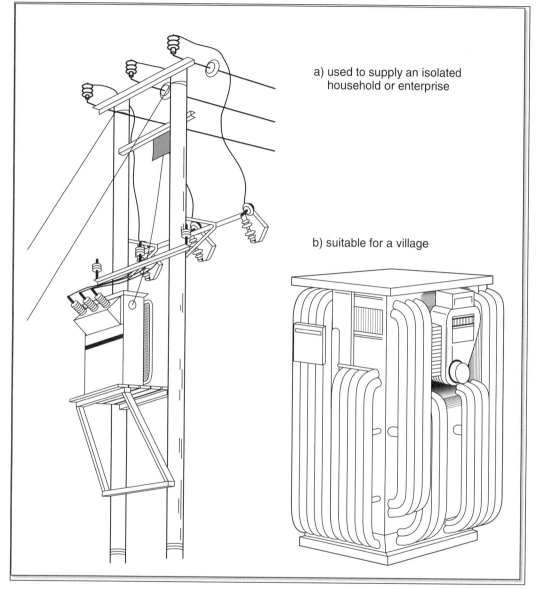

a) used to supply an isolated
household or enterprise

b) suitable for a village

national level by the electricity utility which is either a public or private company. Electricity prices are regulated by the government. In some cases the private generation of electricity has been allowed – usually by industries which need large quantities of electricity (e.g. agro-processing or mines) and sometimes by private individuals (e.g. remote farms). It has usually been unlawful for private generators to sell power to other consumers. However, for a number of reasons, the monopoly position of utilities is being lost and governments are under pressure from within their own countries and from external sources to de-regulate

---

Box 3.1: How electricity is managed in different countries

In South Africa, the government nominates the Electricity Council, which in turn appoints members of the Board of Electricity Supply Commission of South Africa (ESKOM), the electricity utility. ESKOM sets prices without government interference.

In the Philippines, the state-owned utility, National Power Corporation (NPC), co-exists with 282 smaller utilities, of which 194 are privately or municipally owned and the remaining 88 are in the co-operative sector.

In Thailand, the generation and transmission of electricity throughout the country is the responsibility of the Electricity Generating Authority of Thailand (EGAT), while distribution to consumers is the responsibility of two other authorities.

In South Korea, the Korea Electric Power Corporation (KEPCO) is a government invested enterprise which operates the sole electric power system, including generation, transmission and distribution.

The West African state of Liberia is an example of the private sector complementing the public sector electric utility. The state-owned Liberia Electricity Corporation (LEC) supplies power to the country and foreign concessionaires supply power to industry as well as other areas.

In the Indian state of Karnataka, electricity generation (i.e. planning, development and operations) is the responsibility of a government company, the Karnataka Power Corporation Limited.

---

the sector. These changes are expected to bring increased access to electricity as well as investment in more modern plant.

Cost of grid electricity to the consumer

Connection fees

These fees vary depending upon what is included in the costs, e.g. cables taking the supply to the consumer or transformers (see Table 3.1). Fees range from less than US$20 up to US$4000. The level of payments can also vary because of the different ways utilities charge customers. Sometimes the utility sets the price at less than real costs to stimulate the market. Sometimes the government provides a direct subsidy. Sharing the costs with other consumers (if they are close enough) can reduce the payments.

Table 3.1: Service connection cost breakdown for Sri Lanka (1992) and Botswana (1994)

Cost element	Sri Lanka (US$)	Botswana (US$)
Meter and installation	27	175
Cable per metre	0.16	7.5
Additional poles	50	80

The cost of wiring the household or micro-enterprise to the standard required by the utility may not be included in the

Figure 3.3: Residential tariff structure in Thailand

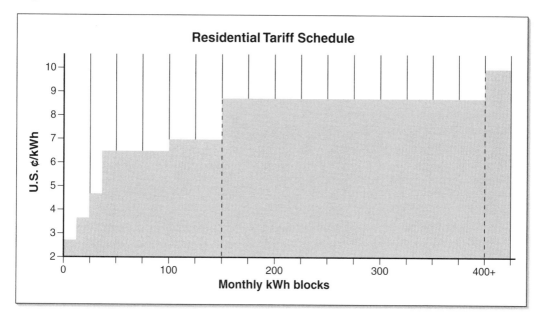

connection fees, and is the consumer's responsibility. In Malawi it costs US$100 to wire a house, which is more than ten times the connection fee.

In some countries, for safety reasons, households with traditional thatched-roof houses are not allowed an electricity supply because they do not have a permanent watertight roof. In Tanzania, for example, the average cost of upgrading and connecting a house to the standard required by TANESCO is about US$250. However, in Bangladesh it costs only US$4 and there is no connection charge if the household or micro-enterprise is within 30 metres of the distribution line for electricity.

Tariffs

The utility recovers its investment and operating costs through the price it charges its customers. Each utility has its own tariff structure, and tariffs differ from country to country. Example 3.1 gives an example of the tariff structure used in South Africa.

There may be different tariffs for large customers (such as manufacturing industries) and small customers (such as households and micro-enterprises). Urban areas may pay a different rate than rural areas. The government may also provide direct subsidies. Customers are normally classified into different groups, e.g. (1) Domestic (i.e. households), (2) General purpose (business or micro-enterprise), (3) Commercial and (4) Large industries. It is not unusual for different categories of customers to pay a different price per unit (kWh) of electricity (see Figure 3.3).

To enable low-income households to have access to electricity a special tariff, sometimes called a lifeline tariff, is used. For example, in Nepal a rural electrification project charges US$0.34 for 25W, US$0.7 for 50W and US$1.90 for 250W. A physical device, known as a load limiter, regulates the amount of electricity supplied. If the current exceeds a specific value, the load limiter automatically disconnects the supply. Some types of load limiter have to

---

Example 3.1: Tariff structures: example from South Africa

The Electricity Supply Commission of South Africa (ESKOM) used the following tariff structure in 1995:

Business rate: for customers who own small businesses in urban areas with an installed capacity of not more than 80kW.

Land rate: for agricultural and domestic purposes, small businesses, schools, clinics and water pumps in rural areas, with an installed capacity of less than 80kVA.

Home power: for customers within an area marked for residential use or a group of dwellings, churches, halls and old-age homes.

Ruralflex: for all 3-phase rural customers, who take supply from 400V to 220V. In order to qualify for this tariff, consumption has to be shifted to specified time periods, outside high peak demand times. This is a strategy to use the utility's surplus generating capacity, which is profitable for the utility and can be advantageous to consumers as well. For example, a dairy could shift its bottle washing, using electrically heated water, to night-time, or a battery recharging business could operate at night.

---

be reset manually, while others work automatically when the overload is removed by switching off an electrical appliance. The customer is charged a fixed fee irrespective of the total amount of energy consumed.

If a micro-enterprise is being run from home, the utility's tariff structure needs careful scrutiny to ensure that the most favourable rate is being used. This may require two meters and separate lines for the household and micro-enterprise and these investment costs will also need to be taken into account. However, utilities may not be prepared to split the bills if the total consumption is small because the administrative overheads would be too high.

Paying for electricity consumption

The utility bills the consumer for the amount of electricity used over a set period of time, for example, once a month, every 3 months, or annually. The bill is worked out on the basis of a reading from the meter installed at the household or micro-enterprise. The amount is usually expressed in terms of kWh. Failure to pay the bill can result in the consumer being disconnected from the supply. The utility usually demands a high fee for reconnection.

Many consumers find it difficult to match their cash flow to utility billing patterns and many utilities are now introducing pre-payment cards. The consumer buys a card, which entitles her to a fixed quantity of electricity (or number of units). The card is inserted into the meter and the electricity supply runs until all the units have been consumed. Inserting a new card in the meter reconnects the supply. The system is cheaper for the utility to administer and ensures payment, and the consumer is able to match her purchase of electricity to her cash income.

Lobbying for grid connection

This section explains how a utility decides where and when to extend the grid and

---

Box 3.2: Criteria for selecting a village for grid connection

In Thailand the PEA (the authority responsible for rural electrification) makes an initial priority ranking of the villages in a particular area for grid connection based on the following criteria:

○ Receipt of request for electrification, usually with a letter of support from the Governor
○ Village must be less than 15km from the grid (otherwise it may qualify for a mini-grid based on micro-hydro)
○ Distance of village from main road
○ Village size, number of people and households
○ Number of expected initial customers and average investment required per household
○ Power equivalent of existing machines and other energy sources
○ Number of project construction works and cost of investment per household
○ Number of commercial establishments (including economic and social status, number of temples, schools, rice mills, libraries, shops, health centres, co-operatives, water pumping plants, repair shops, water works, irrigation, businesses and cottage industries)
○ Number of existing infrastructure facilities
○ Status of the village, such as the existence of a local political office or sub-district committee, local community centre, recognition of the importance of the village to national security or the existence of development projects undertaken by government agencies.

---

how a community might influence this process.

The decision by a utility to connect a community to the grid is usually based on socio-economic considerations, which may differ from country to country. Therefore, each utility uses its own criteria. Sometimes the government asks the utility to bring electricity to a specific area in order to encourage development. Box 3.2 gives an example of the criteria used for rural electrification in Thailand. Generally, the utility wants to be assured that enough electricity will be sold in the community to make the cost of building the power lines to the village worthwhile. There should also be some visible level of development (e.g. schools, clinic or hospital, shops, market, lodge, village water supply unit and agricultural activities). The infrastructure (the buildings and facilities) can be a sign to the utility that there is a potential demand for electricity.

In order to make a decision about extending the grid, the utility usually wants some general information about a community, such as the number of potential customers, how close together the houses are (density), what economic activities the community is involved in, and if there are any new development projects that are likely to use electricity. It is important to ensure that both women's and men's interests and activities are taken into account. Women might find it advantageous to group together to ensure that their voices are heard.

The utility also has specific questions about households and micro-enterprises which include: maximum possible number of households to be connected; the kind of work done by the head of the household; monthly income; sources of energy used and application (e.g. lighting, heating, cooking); number of lights and their type; energy costs per month;

existing electric appliances; how much a household can afford to pay, both for a connection and per month, for electricity. It may also consider micro-enterprises (e.g. dairies, grain-mills, cafés, hair salons); how many days in a week the micro-enterprises are open and how long the working day is. Utilities are not always sensitive to collecting data in a manner that reflects women's and men's activities within their households and cummunities. Women need to raise the issue when the utility makes a preliminary visit to prepare the community for data collection (see Chapter 7).

The utility needs data to plan towards meeting present needs and to estimate future demands and the rate at which demand is likely to grow. The grid is most likely to be extended to areas where there is a high population density and consequently a high demand.

Since a large number of people do not have electricity, utilities are under tremendous pressure from communities and politicians for grid extension. Communities therefore need to lobby the utility. This requires a well-organized campaign to demonstrate to the utility that the community is serious about its desire for a connection, is aware of the costs involved and has the ability to pay. First, it is important to know what criteria the utility uses to consider extending the grid and to use this information when drawing up the proposal. The proposal should include information on how many people would like to be connected, for what purposes, and an indication of their consumption level with, if possible, an estimate of how the demand is likely to grow during the five years after connection. It is important that women play an active role in this communal decision-making so that their wishes are made clear and are included in the proposal. Clearly, any such initiative will have

more strength if it comes from an official body such as a village council and has the support of the local MP or district administrator. This support should be sought before approaching the utility. Contributions to be provided by the community should also be included in the proposal as they help to demonstrate seriousness of intent; for example, a commitment to a certain number of connections. Collection of payments is expensive for utilities and this is one of the reasons that they are often reluctant to undertake rural electrification. The community can therefore offer to assist the utility in the collection of fees. Contributions do not have to be cash but can be practical offers of help, for example, assisting in the erection of poles for carrying the power lines. In Thailand, the body responsible for rural electrification rents rooms from local people for its staff involved in the system installation, which helps keep their costs down. Local people have also been hired at market rates to work on installation. This has put money into the local economy and increased people's ability to pay for the service. Contributions by local communities are among the reasons why Thailand has achieved high levels of rural electrification.

The utility will consider the proposal from a specific village only if the grid is already in the area or it is intended to move into that district or region soon. If grid extension is planned for a date in the distant future or if the community is located in a region where the terrain makes it unlikely that there is any prospect of joining the national grid, then alternatives such as the stand-alone options may be possible. These options could be evaluated with the help of the utility, which may regard this as a useful opportunity to stimulate demand to a sufficient level so that future grid extension becomes feasible.

Case study: Financing rural electrification: the case of Zimbabwe

The Zimbabwe Electricity Supply Authority (ZESA) has three financing schemes for rural electrification:

1. *The Rural Institutions Revolving Fund.* The German Development Agency GTZ provide financial support to ZESA for a loan fund to enable institutions, such as schools, clinics, clubs, colleges and police stations, to borrow money at significantly below the market rate (17% compared to 30% in July 1998).

2. *The Rural Electrification Guarantee Scheme.* This loan fund assists communities with a regular source of income to pay for the connection fee. Again, interest rates are pegged below market rates.

3. *The Funds Matching Scheme.* The community pays half of the full electrification work done by ZESA and the other half is paid by the Rural Electrification Fund. Any community with at least 100 beneficiaries is eligible for funds.

Comparing costs of grid electricity with stand-alone systems

The cost of grid connection is a major determinant of whether or not a household or micro-enterprise will apply for a supply. For those considering a stand-alone system, comparing the costs of different options (both electrical and non-electrical) is one of the main criteria of selection. In some cases, consumers may also want to evaluate the cost of stand-alone systems compared with a grid connection.

For households and for most micro-enterprises, a comparison of costs can be made simply on the basis of expenditure over a period of time (see Chapter 7). Community schemes are more complex to cost since they involve much larger outlays of money, some of which may have to be borrowed, and there will also be income coming in. This book uses a simple calculation for households or micro-enterprises. For community-size schemes, expert help is recommended for calculating costs.

Costs for comparing simple schemes can be broken down into three components:

○ Initial cost of grid connection or RPS, which includes any money for transportation and installation of the RPS.

○ Annual recurrent costs, the money paid to the utility for electricity consumed or the money for operation, fuel, other inputs (such as battery fluid), maintenance and repair.

○ Investment costs, the interest on any loans, dividends, fees to government.

As well as the costs, the benefits and disadvantages of each system need to be assessed. There is no easy way to assign monetary values to some of these, for example noise from a generator or the convenience of electric light compared to candles or the lack of smoke when cooking on an electric hotplate. People have to make decisions based on their own criteria and the value they put on having access to electricity. For example, villagers in Mizque and Aiquille in rural Bolivia were prepared to pay four to five times as much for their electricity from a micro-hydro scheme as consumers in comparable grid-connected villages paid elsewhere in the country.

The costs of providing electricity are highly site specific as can be seen in Figure 3.4, which shows the cost of electricity from three different systems delivered to

Figure 3.4: Comparison of relative costs for electricity at three locations in Namibia

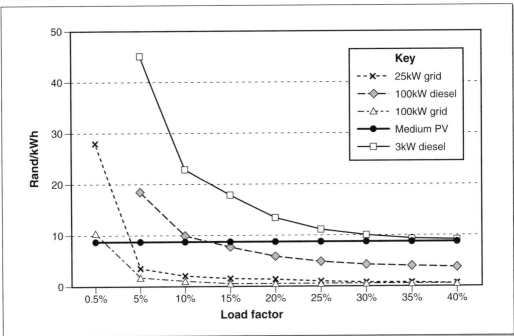

a) 10km from the grid in Owambo

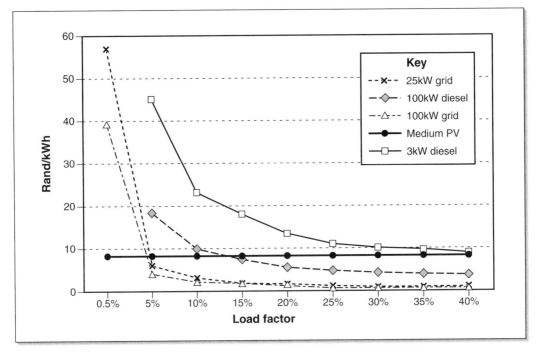

b) 10km from the grid in Okavango West

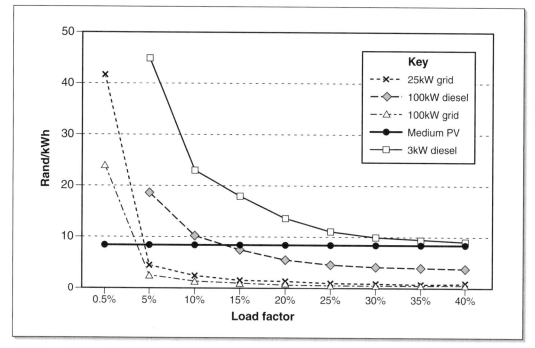

c) 10km from the grid in Okavango East

Source: Solar Energy for Rural Communities: The Case of Namibia, G. Yaron, T. Forbes Irving and S. Jansson (IT Publications) 1994

Example 3.2: The cost of lighting a single room: kerosene compared with solar electricity

Energy source	Kerosene	Solar electricity
Equipment required	Pressure lamp, mantles and fuel	'Neste Magic Lantern' consisting of: 6Wp module lead acid battery 7W lamp mount
First cost	Pressure lamp – US$30	All equipment: US$160
Annual recurring cost	Fuel and mantles: US$60–100 per year	Battery/tube replacements: US$20 per year
Total outlay after three years	US$210–330	US$220

Prices are in 1995 US dollars, equipment and kerosene retail prices based on availability in Nairobi
Source: Solar Electric Systems for Africa, Hankins 1995

three locations in Namibia, each 10km from the grid. Costs also need to be compared with other means of providing the service. Example 3.2 compares the use of solar electricity and kerosene for lighting a single room over a 3-year period. The values used here are from Nairobi (Kenya) in 1995; however, this approach can be used anywhere by substituting local values into the table.

In this example it would take between two and four years (depending on the price of kerosene) for the benefits of the rather high initial investment in the solar lighting system to be felt financially. However, this does not take into account other benefits which have not been quantified: the greater convenience and safety, as well as the higher quality of light from the solar lantern.

Fluctuations in demand and how they influence system selection

The use of electricity is not constant over a 24-hour period. Generally, households want electricity in the evenings, for lighting and televisions, whereas micro-enterprises want power during the day. Even during these two periods there is a fluctuation in demand, as people switch equipment on and off. Some appliances, such as refrigerators, switch themselves on and off, while other equipment (such as photocopiers and fax machines) is left on standby for more efficient operation and so draws some power even when not in use. These fluctuations in demand have to be taken into account when selecting the system.

Some generating systems produce electricity on demand (diesel generators for example) and so respond well to fluctuations in demand. Other systems, for example micro-hydro systems, produce electricity continuously, which may be wasted in the middle of the night or during the day when people work in the fields. It is a good idea to try to use this 'wasted' electricity for productive tasks (e.g. for charging batteries or for running equipment such as grinding machines),

which will help to spread the cost of the investment over more users.

Example 3.3 introduces the concepts of peak (maximum demand) and base loads (continuously operating demand). The difference between the peak power demand and the base load has a significant effect on the cost of the supply system. If the electricity comes from the grid it is the utility's problem and they adopt a number of management strategies to spread the demand as evenly as possible. However, for households, micro-enterprises and communities managing their own electricity supply, it is a problem which has to be considered carefully since it has serious implications for system costs. The greater the difference between the peak and base loads, the greater the risk for unnecessary investment costs. Most stand-alone systems come in modularized form. The choice then has to be made whether to buy a system which meets the peak demand, irrespective of cost, or to buy a smaller system and adopt some load management strategies, such as switching off non-essential equipment, until the load matches supply capabilities. (The latter is a practice known as load-shedding, which is used by the large utilities.) For households and micro-enterprises, the difference between peak and base loads may not be great enough to warrant any changes to the system. In some cases, peaks in the load could be met by batteries, which can be recharged during periods of low demand.

Conclusion

Grid connection has a number of benefits for the end-user. It is convenient because the user does not have to worry about production of electricity and maintenance of the system, since this is the responsibility of the utility. The supply from the grid should be reliable (where the system capacity is sufficient) and the voltage reasonably constant. An important disadvantage in some countries is that the costs of connection, especially in rural areas, is too high. For many people around the world, access to grid-based electricity is still a remote prospect. This, linked with the reforms of utilities to allow more private supply of electricity, is encouraging people to examine the possibility of using stand-alone systems for the generation of electricity. In some countries, the grid supply is highly unreliable, with frequent power cuts and reduced voltages (brown-outs), again causing people to consider stand-alone systems as back-ups. The options for stand-alone generation are described in the next chapter.

Example 3.3: Peak and base loads

A household has three 60W light bulbs, a television (rated at 80W) and a refrigerator (rated at 300W). The lights are turned on after sunset. One or two lights are left on during the night for safety reasons. The Figure below shows the average use of energy during a 24-hour period. The television is used for only 4 hours in the evening. The refrigerator is in use for the whole 24-hour period, however the motor automatically switches on and off, resulting in it using energy only 50% of the time. This means that when it is 'on', its power demand is 300W, but during 1 hour it only needs $300 \times 1 \times 0.5 = 150$Wh of energy.

The total use of energy over a 24-hour period is represented in Figure 3.5 by the shaded area which is approximately 5.5kWh of electrical energy. Equipment which is running continuously provides a *base load* which indicates the minimum power demand that the generating equipment has to meet. In this example the refrigerator during the daylight hours is the base load. The required power is then about 150W. The peak use is in the evening when the light bulbs and the television are on. Then the maximum or *peak* power needed is about 400W.

Figure 3.5: Total use of electric energy in a household for a 24-hour period

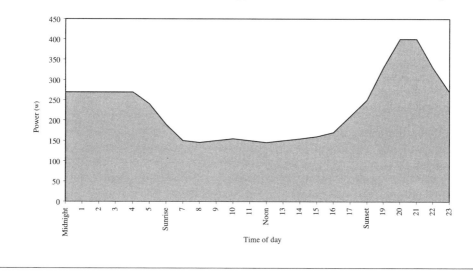

4
Stand-alone generation of electricity

Introduction

THIS CHAPTER DESCRIBES in a systematic way a number of options for stand-alone production of electricity and for whom they are most appropriate. The technical descriptions are kept to a minimum but are sufficient to allow for an initial selection of options for further study. A brief description is given of how each option works, the resources required and the expertise needed.[2] The system reliability and maintenance requirements, including what tasks are possible at community level, are also covered. Some indications of equipment and operating costs are given; however, in reality these are very site specific and can be influenced by transport costs and local taxation systems. These locally variable factors can affect the relative prices of different technologies and hence influence the selection of one technology over another. The increasing interest in renewable energies means that new developments are constantly appearing on the market, which can lead to cost reductions. On the other hand, fluctuations in local currencies can reduce these benefits. It is therefore very difficult to give general cost data that will be relevant for use at a particular location.

All energy systems have environmental impacts. In general, small-scale renewable energy systems can be said to have lower impacts than conventional systems based on fossil fuels, large hydro and nuclear power. An indication of the environmental impacts of system operation are given for each technology. Impacts are usually felt locally at the site of generation for small-scale systems, and for large systems used with grid electricity environmental impacts of generation are also felt some distance away. It is also important to consider the impacts of any energy forms that are being replaced by the use of electricity. For example, electric lighting is of a higher quality than that from oil lamps and so eye strain (health effect) is less for the former. If electric cooking is possible, women could benefit significantly in terms of their health (reduced lung and eye diseases) if this replaces fuelwood.

One of the disadvantages of stand-alone systems is that they are susceptible to interruptions in the supply of the energy resource. The sun does not shine at night when households need electricity and there are cloudy days. The wind is intermittent. Streams and rivers are subject to seasonal fluctuations in flow. Diesel supplies do not always arrive. To overcome the problems of energy resource supply, it is common to use RPS in combination with batteries. Batteries act as a means of electrical energy storage for use when the renewable energy resource is not available, and, in some places, batteries are people's only access to a supply

---

2 Expertise is defined as low (little education and brief training), medium (good basic education and formal training) and high (good technical education).

of electricity. In fact businesses offering battery-charging services can be found all over the world and those using renewable energy resources, particularly solar energy, are gaining in popularity. In view of the important role batteries play in the stand-alone supply of electricity, a separate section is devoted to them.

Diesel generators

Introduction

Diesel generating sets are used in urban and remote areas for a number of purposes:

○ To augment (increase) the grid power supply;
○ As stand-by generators, which means that they are automatically or manually switched on when the usual electricity supply is cut off or insufficient;
○ As the only means of electricity supply, to individual households, micro-enterprises or communities.

How diesel generators work

A diesel engine burns diesel fuel in an enclosed space (the cylinder). The hot gases expand and push down a cylinder and the attached piston rod. This linear motion is converted into rotating motion by the crank, which in turn drives a dynamo or alternator to generate electricity. In this manner stored chemical energy in the fuel is converted into electrical energy. The engine and dynamo/alternator system are referred to as a diesel generator or gen-set.

There are various types of generators on the market, which are available in the size range of interest (5kW to 100kW) for households, micro-enterprises and small communities.

Figure 4.1: Typical diesel generator set rated at 15kW

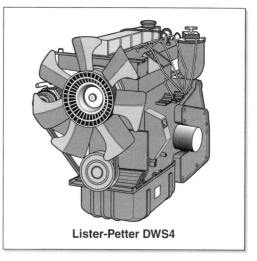

Lister-Petter DWS4

Diesel engines are sold at a rated (or maximum) power and speed (for example 5kW at 3000 rpm (revolutions per minute)). The size of the engine chosen will depend upon whether it is to be operated intermittently or continuously (for longer than an hour). For electricity generation, the latter is more common, in which case the engine should not be operated at its rated (maximum) power, since this shortens engine life and increases costs. A guideline for selecting engine size is that during continuous operation the power is around 20% less than its rated power. Manufacturers will usually quote figures both for rated power and continuous operation. The latter needs to be used for calculation of the power output.

Diesel engines should be operated as near to full load as possible. Running for long periods at low loads, particularly at zero load (idling), creates engine deposit build-ups (coking) and produces smokier exhaust than at full load. This wastes fuel through inefficient combustion and increases maintenance and repair costs.

Larger diesel engines tend to be more fuel efficient than smaller ones.

Therefore, if a number of households or businesses within an area require electricity, and diesel is the preferred option, it is better to consider a mini-grid based on one large engine than several decentralized smaller ones. This also offers financial advantages: the single larger engine will run more efficiently and will therefore cost less to operate; it will probably also last longer, resulting in deferred long-term reinvestment costs.

Diesels need a battery for initial start up. The battery is then recharged during operation. The standard battery employed for this purpose is not suitable as a back-up for periods without diesel fuel or during engine repair.

Costs

A diesel generator rated at 10kVA (a typical value in many rural areas in developing countries) costs about US$4500 in Europe at the factory gate. Therefore, the cost of transportation needs to be included in initial costings, as does a suitable building for housing the generator set and batteries, as well as a concrete foundation on which to mount and bolt the engine. Consideration also needs to be given to fuel storage, particularly in more isolated locations where supply is erratic. Diesel fuel is inflammable and so it needs to be stored in appropriate leak-proof containers (oil drums) in a secure location, where smoking should be strictly forbidden to prevent fires and explosions.

Operating costs include diesel fuel, lubrication oil and, if appropriate, batteries. In the interests of fuel efficiency and keeping running costs down, the engine should be run near to its optimum speed and as close to full load as possible. This also helps to preserve the lifetime of the engine and minimize maintenance costs.

Resources required

The resource required is diesel fuel. The lubrication oil and the battery fluid need to be topped-up from time to time. Spare parts availability needs to be checked and this may influence the selection of the engine type. Diesel is normally available at petrol stations in towns and cities, although availability in rural areas can be sporadic.

Diesel engines produce a lot of heat and to protect the engine it needs to be cooled. Small engines rely on features built into their design (fins) to conduct the heat away. In high ambient temperatures, a fan may also be needed. The fins need to be cleaned from time to time to ensure good functioning. Larger engines use water for cooling. Although the cooling water is in a closed circuit, it does need topping up from time to time. At high altitudes where temperatures drop below freezing, anti-freeze will need to be added to the cooling water.

Users

Small diesel generators are suitable for individuals for home or workplace use. Larger sized systems can be jointly owned and operated as part of a mini-grid. Diesels are also used as back-up systems for the national grid or integrated with other RPS.

Reliability, maintenance and safety

This is a mature technology, which is universally available. Diesel generators are robust and simple to control but they require simple routine maintenance on a regular basis. This can be learnt by anyone, even without any technical knowledge. Manufacturers provide service instructions which should be followed.

Table 4.1: Summary of advantages and disadvantages of diesel generators

Advantages	Disadvantages
They are readily available on the market; The spare parts are usually available in major centres; Expertise in operation and maintenance widely available; Wide range of power outputs – therefore flexibility in matching present demand and future growth.	Supply of diesel fuel can be expensive if the fuel has to be transported over a long distance; Fuel supply can be unreliable, especially in more remote areas; Uses fossil fuels – therefore increases greenhouse effect; Batteries may be required as a back-up and need storage space; Diesel generators are noisy and produce smelly exhaust gases.

For example, they will recommend how frequently the oil and oil filter should be changed. From time to time, a more thorough servicing carried out by a diesel mechanic will be needed. The need for major maintenance can be kept to a minimum by operating the engine at reasonable loads and speeds.

The operator should ensure that there is sufficient fuel in the tank and in particular the level of lubrication oil should be checked once a week. This is a simple task and requires no special skills. Lack of lubrication due to insufficient oil in the sump is one of the most common causes of diesel engine failure. Some engine manufacturers now include an automatic cutout if the lubrication oil level drops to a dangerous level. The sump needs to be drained from time to time and the oil and oil filter replaced. The fuel filter also needs to be replaced periodically. Vibration from the engine during operation causes nuts and bolts to work loose. These need to be checked regularly and tightened to safeguard the engine.

If well looked after, diesel generators should have a lifetime of 10–15 years, but there are many diesel engines around the world which have been in operation for much longer than this.

Diesel engines have moving parts which are mainly enclosed; however, care needs to be taken that loose clothing does not get caught in exposed areas. Maintenance should only be carried out with the engine switched off. The exhaust pipe is hot and can cause severe burns so it should be enclosed in a mesh guard. Although diesel fuel does not cause burns if it comes into contact with the skin, it should be washed off as soon as possible and washing hands is particularly recommended before eating.

Expertise needed

For operation and routine maintenance, after brief instruction, no special skills are required.

Environmental impacts

Diesel engines are noisy, they use diesel fuel which is a fossil fuel and its use therefore contributes to the greenhouse effect and the exhaust is smoky since the gases produced during combustion contain a large amount of particulate matter. The lower the load and the lower the speed at which the engine runs, the higher the level of

Case study: Village electrification by privately owned diesel generators in Yemen

Yemen is almost totally electrified. Private electricity generation is allowed. In areas where there is no grid supply, private diesel generators are used. The average generator size is about 5kW. Since 1991 about 460 000 families have obtained their electricity from private suppliers. The service is provided typically for 5–6 hours daily and charges are usually based on the number of lights.

The utility ensures the safety of the power supply, making inspections from time to time. Connections from house to house are very simple.

Because the facility is proving popular, owners of the diesel generators have had to buy larger generators to be able to connect more households to their mini-grids.

Source: Dr E.T. Ferguson, MacFergus BV, The Netherlands

particulates in the exhaust. The noise and pollution mean that the location of the engine relative to dwellings needs careful consideration.

Diesel engines can also be run on a range of biomass-derived fuels, for example, vegetable oils such as jatropha (black soap) and sunflower oil, biogas and producer gas (the latter two are described later in this chapter). Using biomass-derived fuels does not lead to the increase of greenhouse gases.

Conclusion

Diesel generators are a tried and tested option suitable for providing electricity at all levels.

Micro-hydro power

Introduction

Hydro power uses the energy of falling water, or fast-flowing rivers. The rivers must flow through steep areas where the water descends between 1.5 and 400 metres. The distance the water descends is known as the head.

Hydro power plants come in a range of sizes: from very large plants (above 1000kW) to small (500–1000kW), to mini (100–500kW) to micro plants (below 100kW). Unlike large-scale hydro power plants, micro-hydro does not require massive damming of the river. Plants can be constructed to supply from 3kW up to 100kW, which is the range of interest to households and micro-enterprises.

There are also small battery-charging systems which include a controller, generator and turbine. These can work on heads as low as 0.75 metres, but 8 metres is more appropriate. They cost around US$450 and are capable of producing power at a lower cost than a PV system with the same output.

Hydro power has been used for many years in many countries. Micro-hydro is most suitable where there is sufficient water and the grid extension is impracticable, due to the terrain, or is too expensive. To be financially viable there must usually be a demand for electricity during the day from productive industry, such as a metalworking shop or sawmill, the demand from households alone is insufficient to repay the capital costs. Micro-hydro schemes can also be integrated with other uses of water such as irrigation, fish farming, provision of drinking water and tourism.

Micro-hydro schemes are not likely to be attractive where:

Figure 4.2: Components of a micro-hydro scheme

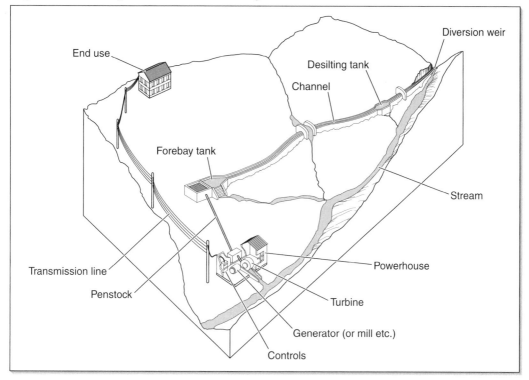

- The terrain is flat, since civil works costs will be too high (unless it is linked to an irrigation or drinking water scheme);
- Streams have their source in low rainfall areas.

How micro-hydro systems work

The components of a micro-hydro scheme are usually split into two categories: the civil works, which means buildings and other structures; and the electro-mechanical parts, which means the machines and electrical equipment.

The Figures 4.2 and 4.3 show the features of a micro-hydro scheme and some common layouts.

The plant consists of a weir which diverts water from the river through a channel to a desilting tank. This desilting (or settling) tank, allows rocks and other debris to settle so that when the water flows into the turbine it contains no dirt which could damage the equipment. The channel (or canal) leads from the settling tank into the forebay tank which is used to remove any floating debris, such as leaves. From there the water passes to the power house through the penstock (the pipe which carries the water to the turbine). In the power house there is a turbine, a generator and a governor – the control mechanism which keeps the generator operating smoothly. The governor can either control the flow of water to the turbine (matching power with demand) or it can dump excess power into water-cooled electrical elements, which absorb it. The latter is known as a load controller and is usually used in preference to flow

Figure 4.3: Common layouts for micro-hydro schemes

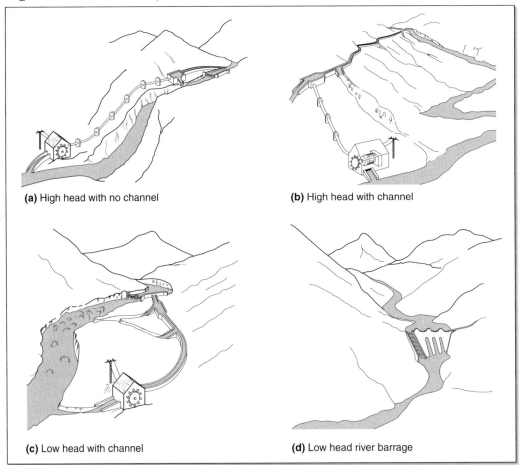

(a) High head with no channel

(b) High head with channel

(c) Low head with channel

(d) Low head river barrage

control since it offers greater reliability and accuracy at a lower cost. Once the water has been through the turbine, it is returned to the stream through a channel known as a tailrace.

Main types of turbine available

There are several different turbine types. Selection is usually made on the basis of the height of water (the head) and the flow at the site of installation. The Pelton, Francis, Kaplan and Crossflow are the most commonly used turbines (see Figure 4.4).

Pelton
This machine is used where there are high heads (greater than 100m). The water jet strikes the concave side of a pair of spoon-shaped buckets and leaves on either side of the wheel (Figure 4.4a). Pelton turbines are suitable for local manufacture which can make them low cost. Pelton turbines are robust and more tolerant of silt and debris than most other types.

Francis
This is a radial-flow turbine, which can be designed to cover a wide range of head and flow conditions (Figure 4.4b). Heads,

Figure 4.4: Main types of turbines

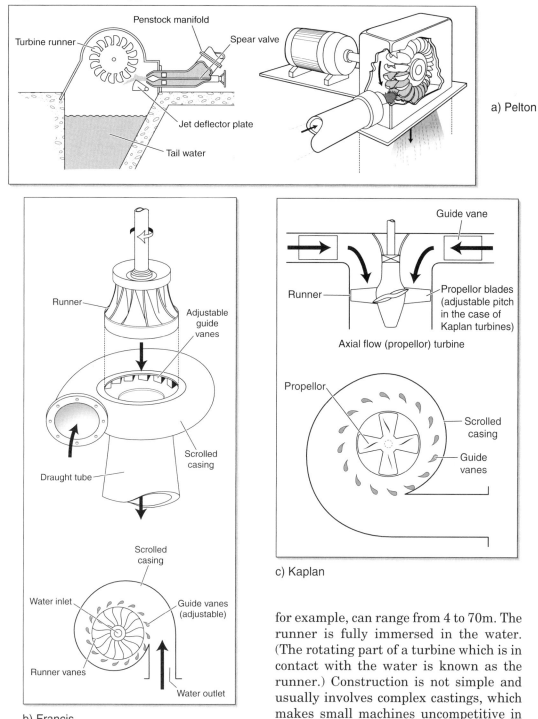

a) Pelton

b) Francis

c) Kaplan

for example, can range from 4 to 70m. The runner is fully immersed in the water. (The rotating part of a turbine which is in contact with the water is known as the runner.) Construction is not simple and usually involves complex castings, which makes small machines uncompetitive in some countries. Francis machines are

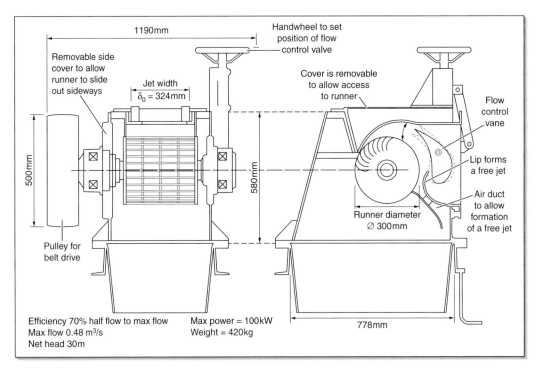

d) Crossflow

often designed specifically for one site, a practice which makes them expensive. Regular removal of silt and debris are required to avoid rapid wear.

Kaplan
The Kaplan or axial-flow turbine consists of a propeller-shaped runner rotating in a tubular case (Figure 4.4c). Although the efficiency of this type of turbine can be high, the cost and complexity can also be high. However, there are simplified designs available on the market and under development. Heads usually range from 2m to 10m. Good control of silt and debris is necessary to avoid wear and blockages.

Crossflow (Mitchell-Banki)
This turbine is used at head sites of 7–60m. The water is directed along the full length of the runner and it strikes the turbine blades both as it enters and as it leaves the turbine (Figure 4.4d). The design is popular in developing countries

because of its ease of manufacture in simple workshops. Careful design can lead to high part-load efficiencies at reasonable cost, which are not found with other turbine designs.

Costs

Investment costs for micro-hydro are very site specific. They depend on the location and the capacity of the plant. Surveying, designing, specifying and supervising installation all need expert inputs, which can be expensive. Added to these costs are those for infrastructure, equipment, electricity transmission and distribution. Equipment for the plant costs about 30% of the total investment.

In 1994, a small locally manufactured micro-hydro system in Nepal cost US$1000 per kW installed. A locally manufactured micro-hydro in Argentina cost US$3576 per kW installed including distribution. Imported equipment would cost US$8000–20 000 per kW installed. For micro-hydro systems, small economies of scale are possible, so that the cost per kW decreases slightly with every extra kW installed.

A rough guide for estimating micro-hydro costs is that if the community requires Y kilowatts capacity and the hydro plant is located farther than 100 times Y metres away it is unlikely to be cost-effective. For example, for a village with a 10kW load the site of the hydro plant should not be more than 1km away because the costs of transmission are likely to be unacceptably high.

Although there are no fuel costs with hydro power, and often only a few moving parts, their remote locations and small numbers can lead to unexpectedly high running costs. This is especially true of rehabilitated micro-hydro schemes, where repairs tend to be expensive. Ten per cent of the total capital cost per year gives a reasonable estimate of running costs. Schemes of less than 100kW can be designed to run unattended.

Resources required

Two values need to be estimated to give an indication of the possibilities for hydro power at a particular location: the head (the height at the point of construction the water drops) (m) and the volume of water flowing (m³/s). There are simple methods for estimating the site potential which can give an initial evaluation and do not need high levels of skill to use.

Power (kW) can be estimated from:

$$\text{Power} = 5 \times \text{Flow (m}^3/\text{s)} \times \text{Head (m)}$$

Head and speed of flow should be measured at the end of the dry season to show the likely minimum power output. Clearly, regions in which the seasonal

Figure 4.5: Small turbine capable of small power output from low head source

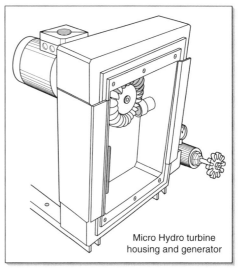

Micro Hydro turbine housing and generator

variations are small are more suitable for micro-hydro applications than those where there are large variations.

Users

Most micro-hydro schemes are built to serve a whole village or number of households or enterprises together. Due to the high costs, systems requiring civil works are rarely constructed for use by a single household or micro-enterprise, except occasionally for very isolated farms where they may be combined with water storage schemes. There are, however, systems which can produce small amounts of power (less than 0.5kW) from a water source and a low head penstock (7m) which, when combined with a battery, can be used for households or micro-enterprises (see Figure 4.5).

Reliability, maintenance and safety

Micro-hydro technology has been in use for a long time in developing countries,

Table 4.2: Summary of advantages and disadvantages of micro-hydro

Advantages	Disadvantages
Low operating and maintenance costs; As long as river flow is constant, power is produced at a fairly constant rate so that there is little need for storage batteries; There are no large dams, avoiding problems such as resettlement of people; Noise levels considerably below diesel generator; Technology is simple and robust; No pollution.	Micro-hydro is a site-specific technology, so suitable sites are required close to locations where power is needed; Once installed the size is fixed. It is not easy to meet growth in demand; In low rainfall periods power output can be severely restricted or zero, so only suitable where there is year-round flow; Advanced engineering skills are needed for design and construction.

especially in Asia and Latin America. Although there are a number of large dams in Africa, the exploitation of micro-hydro sites has been very limited until now.

This technology is considered very reliable, but it requires regular routine checks on a daily, weekly, monthly and annual basis. The emphasis is on ensuring that the flow of water to the turbine is sufficient. The forebay screen needs to be cleared daily of material carried along by the water and should be drained and cleaned on a weekly basis. The channel needs to be checked weekly and the penstock monthly for leaks. The weir intake and channels need to be cleaned of debris every month. Valves and other moving parts need greasing once a month. Sealing leaks and general repairs need to be carried out annually.

Micro-hydro is a robust technology and will give good service for about 20 years without any major new investment. Improvements are continuing with electronic control devices, methods for system sizing and in turbine manufacturing techniques.

Expertise needed

System design requires high levels of expertise. Installation of the civil works (i.e.

weir) requires low to medium skills, while the installation of the turbine and generator requires high skills. This requirement increases with size of the equipment. Low skills are required for operation and medium skills for maintenance. Although unattended operation is possible, someone in the community needs to be familiar with the operating principles and be responsible for regular clearing of debris, checking for leaks and other maintenance tasks.

Environmental impacts

Micro-hydro schemes do not have the negative environmental impacts generally associated with large hydro schemes, e.g. loss of land and population displacement. The total flow of water entering and leaving the micro-hydro system is the same and, as a result, there is no loss of amenity. However, the stretch of water between the entry and exit points is subject to a reduction in flow. This can lead to an increase in women's workload if they have to walk further to collect water for their domestic needs or if it means a relocation of bathing or clothes washing facilities. It is therefore important that women are involved in decisions about the location of the various components of the system.

Case study: Women from the Solomon Islands join together

Women from villages in the western province of the Solomon Islands learned about the production of electricity by micro-hydro systems through a training course organized by the Australian NGO APACE. The women came by canoe to Vavanga to see the unit in operation there, part of the WP Rural Renewable Energy Programme. Topics covered included understanding the micro-hydro system, working as a unified community, planning, empowering women as participants, and women's needs in rural electrification. The women learned the components of the system and how to measure the power available from the river. They were taught terminology such as volts and watts, maintenance and repair, and management. The host women living in Vavanga shared their experiences throughout the whole life of the project from the construction to 'switching on', and told of their co-operation, the hard work, the mishaps, and their joy in the final result.

One and a half years later, a second workshop included women from other provinces and those from the four communities where micro-hydro systems are operating. These women stressed that their involvement is crucial in such endeavours because a unified effort works. Where only men were involved, projects had failed. They wrote a letter to a national newspaper, which was published, supporting policies for rural electrification focused on complete community involvement, including decision-making. Excursions were made to the dam, penstock, turbine, generation house and power house. In Iriri the women saw small businesses made possible by electricity, including the women's bakery.

A crucial component of the rural electrification has been the involvement of the field officer Claudine Lilo, a young local woman. She has been part of the team which visited 116 villages for pre-feasibility studies on their suitability for micro-hydro development. Seven villages have been prioritized for electrification and a 3-month course has been held to train village technicians. Claudine is absolutely crucial to the success of the work as she makes the links between the communities, the provincial government, the technicians and funding agencies. She also helps develop women's small businesses, and so far a bakery, a sewing business and an ice-making facility to preserve the fish catch have been established.

Source: APACE

Poorly designed civil works and excavation may cause severe landslides. This underlines the need for expert assistance in site identification and dam installation.

Conclusion

If appropriate sites are available, it is a reliable, mature technology. Power can be produced at a reasonably constant rate, especially if the river has a steady flow; so the use of batteries can be avoided. Manufacture and use of the technology can easily be adapted to developing countries, where there already exist a number of experienced producers. Overall costs can be low in the case of a community, although high for an individual. Micro-hydro schemes have significantly lower negative

Figure 4.6: Wind turbine components

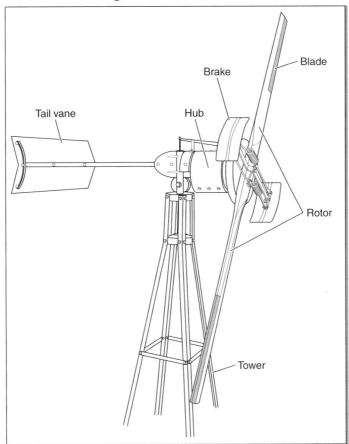

environmental impacts than large schemes.

Wind energy

Introduction

Wind is air which moves, and therefore contains energy. A wind generator, which is often called a wind turbine or windmill, captures this energy. The energy can be used either for electricity generation, and hence a wide range of end uses, or directly for pumping water. This section deals only with wind turbines for generating electricity (which can also be used for running an electric water pump).

Wind turbines come in a range of sizes based on the diameter between the blade tips, which is directly related to the power output. Large and medium turbines are usually used for feeding electricity to a grid. Small wind generators (rated lower than 100kW) are usually not connected to a large grid, but are used for stand-alone generation. This section deals only with small turbines.

Although wind generators can be used in isolation to generate electricity, the intermittent nature of the wind makes this impractical. Wind turbines are therefore usually combined with a battery and

Figure 4.7: Wind generator system components

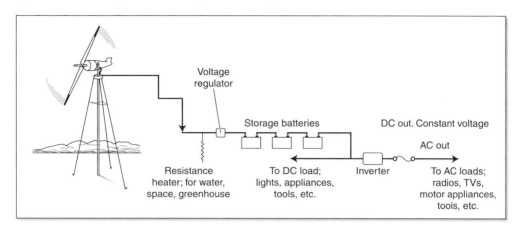

frequently a diesel engine. Increasingly, hybrid systems of wind turbine, solar panel and battery bank are being used in remote locations. This increases the reliability of electricity availability since in many locations there is a strong correlation between sunny windless days and cloudy windy days.

How wind generators work

The wind turbine is made up of a rotor mounted on a tower (see Figure 4.6). The rotor is made up of a number of blades, two or three being most common, mounted on a metal hub. The appearance is similar to an aeroplane propeller. The rotor converts the energy in the wind into the energy of motion of a rotating shaft. This shaft is linked to the generator which produces the electricity. To obtain the maximum amount of energy from the wind, the rotor has to face into the wind. This can be achieved by the use of a tail vane which automatically turns the rotor to the face in the right direction.

Very high wind speeds can damage or break the rotor and the generator can be damaged by over-heating by producing high levels of current due to the rotor

spinning out of control. A safety mechanism is therefore incorporated which shuts down the wind turbine at very high speeds or in storms. There are a number of different approaches to achieve this which either orientate the rotor out of the wind or which stop the rotor turning by a breaking mechanism.

The wind turbine is connected to an electrical generator (Figure 4.7), a battery bank and a charge controller. The charge controller regulates the amount of electricity that goes to the electrical appliances and that which gets stored in the battery. Ensuring that the battery is kept well charged, even in periods of reduced wind, can eliminate the need for a diesel engine. If a diesel engine is incorporated into the system, a special type of programmable inverter will be needed to control the system. If more power is required than is in the battery, the diesel gen-set can be started up automatically. When the diesel is running, the inverter synchronizes the system to ensure that it is running at constant load, which can include recharging the batteries. This ensures the best use of the diesel engine, minimizing fuel consumption and maintenance.

Table 4.3: Indicative output from wind turbines of different diameters at different wind speeds

Average wind speed	Wind turbine rotor diameter			
	1m	2m	3m	5m
3 m/s	0.5	2.5	6	16
4 m/s	1.5	6	15	40
5 m/s	3	12	25	75
6 m/s	4	17	40	110

Note: Energy output is in kWh/week   *Source:* Piggott 1998

Table 4.4: Wind generator applications

Rotor diameter (m)	Rated power (kW)	Rated wind speed (m/s)	Applications
4	1	9	Charging batteries & communication systems
4	5	12	Stand-alone – lighting, refrigeration for household
8	11	11.5	Multi-electrical use, hybrid systems with PV, diesel engine or battery storage
20	100	10.7	Grid extension

Some attention needs to be given to the type of current (AC or DC) supplied by the generator. Some manufacturers design their turbines for use with AC generators. This means that if the turbine is used for charging batteries a rectifier will be needed to convert the AC output to DC. Some manufacturers automatically build a rectifier into their turbines.

The cable from the turbine to the battery needs to be fused to protect the system against faults (e.g. short circuits) which can lead to fires. The fuse should be at the battery end.

The most common parameters manufacturers use to describe their wind generator sizes are rotor diameter and rated power. Rotor diameter is the distance across the circle swept by the tips of the rotor blades, usually measured in metres. A large diameter indicates a potentially substantial output. Table 4.3 gives an indication of how rotor diameter influences output at different wind speeds. The rated power (in watts or kilowatts) is the maximum output of the turbine, which is usually achieved only at high wind speeds (usually quoted as the rated wind speed in m/s). In reality, much less electricity is usually supplied. As a rule of thumb: if a wind turbine is rated at a particular wind speed, and the site has an average wind speed which is half of the rated speed, then one third of the rated power output can be expected on average (see Example 4.1). Another guide is that a reasonable output will be achieved if the site average wind speed is *half* of the wind turbine's rated

Figure 4.8: Small wind generators

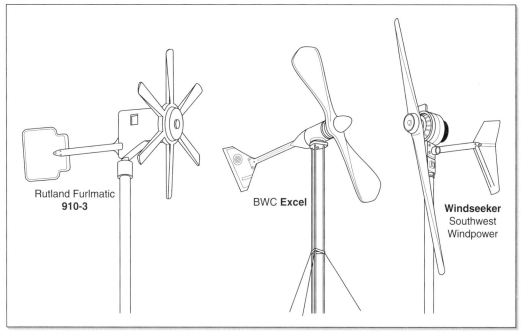

Rutland Furlmatic
910-3

BWC **Excel**

Windseeker
Southwest
Windpower

Example 4.1: Estimating expected power output from a wind turbine

The average wind speed at a given site is 5m/s.

A manufacturer rates the turbine at 3kW at 10m/s.

These conditions meet the rule of thumb, therefore, the estimated expected power output is given by

$1/3 \times 3 \times 24$ = 24kWh per day (or 8760kWh/year)

---

wind speed. If the site value is higher, then an excellent output can be expected.

Table 4.4 gives an indication of the size of turbine appropriate for different applications. The Figure 4.8 shows some small turbines suitable for stand-alone applications.

Costs

Wind generators have high initial costs ranging from US$250 to US$1000/m² rotor

area. Smaller machines usually cost proportionally more per square metre of rotor area. In the mid-1990s a 250W wind generator cost around US$2000 and a 10kW turbine US$20 000 (ex-factory). This does not include the cost of auxiliary equipment. Total costs are strongly linked to the rated wind speed. A wind turbine designed for higher wind speeds will need to be stronger, and have larger components (e.g. generator) to meet the higher loads, and hence will be more expensive. Foundation and installation costs generally come to around 10% of the turbine costs. However, the cost per unit of output may be less for the higher rated turbine, but the investment should be considered only if the site justifies it.

Batteries are needed as a back-up. Selection of the right capacity of batteries for a given system needs detailed wind speed data and an analysis of the demand; the supplier should be able to advise. A rough guideline is that storage

Example 4.2: Influence of wind speed on potential electrical energy output

The average electrical power output (P) for wind generators can be estimated from the following formula:

$$P = 0.2 \times A \times V^3$$

in which A is the rotor area in m² and V is the average annual wind speed in m/s. A wind generator with a rotor area of 20m² (diameter ≈5 metres) is sited in an area with an average annual wind speed of 4m/s. The average power output can be estimated to be:

$$P = 0.2 \times 20 \times 4^3 = 256W$$

However, the same generator located in another area with an average annual wind speed of 6m/s can produce:

$$P = 0.2 \times 20 \times 6^3 = 864W$$

The actual amount of electricity available at the appliances would be less, due to losses in transmission along the cables and conversion in the battery (possibly up to 30%).

Table 4.5: Wind speeds and economic viability of wind generators

Average annual wind speed (m/s)	Economic viability of wind energy use
Below 3 m/s	Not usually economically viable
4–5 m/s	Stand-alone generators may be viable
More than 5 m/s	Viable for stand-alone wind generators
More than 7 m/s	Viable for stand-alone and grid-connected wind generators

Source: Adapted from The Power Guide 1994

sufficient to last between 3 days and a week would generally be adequate for sites with good wind regimes. Batteries may add significantly to the price (up to 30%). The willingness to pay will depend upon the value given to reliability by the user.

Annual operation and maintenance costs are generally estimated to be around 3–5% of the turbine costs (although costs may be much higher if the location is particularly remote). If a diesel engine is part of the system, this adds to the cost. Wind generators are generally economic provided that the minimum monthly average wind speed is more than 4m/s. Many places in the world fail to meet this criterion.

Resources required

If the average wind speed is more than 4m/s and the electricity requirement is small (less than 5kW), then a simple and cheap turbine is possible. Wind speed data may be available from local meteorological stations. They will indicate the average wind speed and also the number of days on which the wind speed is low. This information is important because if wind speed is very variable, production of

Table 4.6: Influence of ground conditions and height above ground on wind speed

Roughness category	Description	Wind speed at height above ground 10 m	20 m
0	Open water	6.9 m/s	7.5 m/s
1	Open areas without significant wind breaks	5.5 m/s	6.2 m/s
2	Open areas with wind breaks (e.g. hedges and bushes)	4.7 m/s	5.5 m/s
3	Urban districts, forests, areas with many wind breaks	3.5 m/s	4.5 m/s

electricity will not be reliable, which increases the back-up storage requirements and hence costs. The readings should have been taken as close to the proposed wind turbine site as possible and the terrain should be similar, otherwise the data will not be appropriate. All airports have good wind data, although they are not always located in the most windy locations so their figures may give a less optimistic impression than is really the case. Agricultural research stations also collect wind data but the measurements are taken closer to the ground than the propeller of the wind turbine is located, again giving a lower potential output than might be produced.

The amount of electricity which can be generated by a wind turbine is highly dependent on the wind speed. The mechanical power depends on the cube of the wind speed. This means, for example, that if the wind speed doubles then the potential power output of the turbine is increased by a factor of eight ($\{2V\}^3 = 2^3 V^3 = 2 \times 2 \times 2 = 8V^3$). Example 4.2 shows how the potential electrical energy output from a wind turbine can be estimated. Table 4.5 indicates how wind speeds influence the options and viability of using wind energy to generate electricity.

The location of the wind generator is very important in terms of maximizing the output. Coastal sites are more likely to have suitable wind regimes than inland sites. However, local topography can enhance wind regimes. There is generally more wind on top of a hill than in the valley bottom. Large buildings and tall trees can block the wind. The generator should therefore stand free from all such barriers. The wind speed also increases with height above the ground. Table 4.6 gives an indication of how ground conditions and height influence wind speed.

Users

Wind turbines are available in sizes appropriate for individual households or micro-enterprises but also for community use. Wind turbines are probably new to many women and they will need extra support in encouraging them to use the technology. There is more widespread experience with windpumps in developing countries and there have been cultural objections to women climbing the towers for routine maintenance of the gearboxes. However, this situation need not arise with wind generators, since routine maintenance occurs at ground level.

Reliability, maintenance and safety

The lifetime of a small wind generator varies between 5 and 10 years. This is a mature, but very complex and sophisticated, technology. In the past there have

Table 4.7: Advantages and disadvantages of wind technology

Advantages	Disadvantages
Much of the technology is well developed; Non-polluting; Experience exists with coupling the technology to back-up systems (e.g. diesel generators and batteries) for periods with no wind.	The initial cost is high; Technology needs batteries; Limited to areas with reasonable winds; Spare parts not always available; Can produce audible noise and interfere with TV signals; Needs regular maintenance by experts.

been problems of reliability with small wind turbines, although there are a number of reliable stand-alone battery charging turbines on the market. There are a number of reasons for this. Turbines which were orginally designed for intermittent holiday home use were expected to function all year round. Also there have been cases reported (fortunately small in number) of blades being shed. This has been attributed to inexperienced people dismantling or tampering with the rotor and hub assembly. The rotor and hub are assembled in the factory so that they are properly balanced and do not wobble in high wind speeds. Therefore, any attempt at servicing the turbine should be left to the experts. Nevertheless it is best to site the turbine away from any living and working areas and frequently used footpaths. This also reduces any irritation caused by the noise from the blades rotating. Parents may be particularly concerned about keeping children away from the area immediately around a wind turbine, so that they are not tempted to climb the tower.

Most problems with small wind turbines are reported to occur in the first year of operation, which should be covered in the manufacturer's warranty. A considerable amount of experience has been gained over the last 20 years and there are several manufacturers with a proven track record. There are also some manufacturers in developing countries, for example, Colombia, China and India. Before a wind turbine is imported, the availability of local skills to service and maintain

the system needs to be checked first.

Once the wind turbine size and output increase the simplest system of just a wind turbine and battery is no longer feasible. Larger outputs are intended for meeting the demands of end-users who require more reliable supplies, such as a small engineering workshop or communities. Above a few kilowatts, it is no longer feasible to simply use a few batteries to smooth out intermittent wind availability. Systems have been tested using diesel engines, as well a hybrid systems with solar, wind and diesel. However, these systems need a skilled operator available and they should be regarded rather more as prototype experimental installations rather than a proven technology.

Expertise needed

Medium to very high engineering skills are needed to install and maintain wind generators. Qualified technicians are needed to replace the wearing parts and to check the system, usually at least twice per year. For the remainder of the time, visual checks from the ground need to be made daily as well as the standard checks on auxilliary equipment, such as batteries and diesel engines. This can be done by the owner after instruction from the installer.

Environmental impacts

With small wind turbines, the main environmental impact relates to noise. The noise generated by the blades 'cutting

> ## Case study: Wind/solar hybrid systems in Fiji
>
> Women from Nabouwalu, Fiji are enthusiastic about their community hybrid power system recently installed in the small town. Nabouwalu is exposed to strong southerly trade winds which makes it an ideal location for wind energy. Eight wind turbines and 40kW solar panels have replaced the very noisy former diesel generators. In fact, the quiet is uncanny! Two 100kVA diesel generators are available for back-up, while 100 batteries store surplus power. The saving at Nabouwalu is F$30 000 annually (US$15 000 in 1998) and the system caters for the government stations, staff quarters, and local shops. The women, like other Pacific people, see an added benefit in using renewables is a contribution to reducing fossil fuel emissions by using less diesel and so helping to curb global warming.
>
> *Source:* Ruth Lechte, ECOWOMAN, Fiji

through the air' can be irritating to some people. Rural areas generally have lower levels of background noise than urban areas, so the introduction of a wind turbine can be intrusive, particularly at night when people are trying to sleep. Careful siting of the wind turbine can reduce nuisance.

Conclusion

Small-scale wind energy is available in sizes suitable for households, micro-enterprises and communities. The technology can be regarded as mature and a number of reliable manufacturers have built up experience which overcomes the earlier criticisms of unreliability. The technology is suitable for manufacture in developing countries, although at present this is not widespread. The high level of technical skills required for the installation of wind systems may be perceived as a barrier to women for access to the technology. However, use of the system requires the same level of skills as the other technologies dealt with in this book, so there are no specific barriers for women's use of wind energy.

Solar electric energy

Introduction

Solar energy is all the energy that reaches the earth from the sun. It can be converted into electrical energy by using solar cell modules (also called photovoltaic or PV cells). Solar electricity has been in use since the 1950s when, due to the high cost, its use was limited to high value applications. However, in the 1980s a number of technical breakthroughs saw the cost of PV cells fall and there was a large increase in use for everyday end uses, particularly for small-scale power demands in remote locations, such as radios, telecommunications and water pumping. Solar electricity systems have found wide applications for powering equipment with low power demands suitable for households and micro-enterprises, such as lighting, radios, TVs, refrigerators, computers and small hand tools. Small portable lanterns capable of giving 3–5 hours lighting and equipment for use at the community level, such as pumps and street lights are also available. Although PV cells are seen to have many potential benefits, they are unable to produce sufficient electricity for cooking.

All regions between latitudes 40°N and 40°S should be suitable for utilizing solar electric systems. Cloudy and rainy days can be accommodated by the use of batteries.

How solar electric energy works

Solar electricity is based on the phenomenon that light falling on certain

Figure 4.9: Components of a solar photovoltaic system

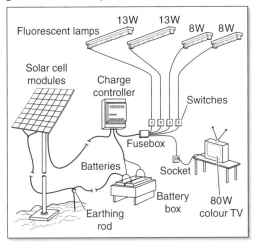

o a set of solar panels, which generates electricity mounted on an appropriate support (see Figure 4.9);

o a charge controller which regulates the amount of electricity going to the battery and appliances;

o an inverter which converts the electricity generated by the array from Direct Current (DC) into Alternating Current (AC) (if DC appliances are not considered an option);

o wiring and fixtures used for putting the system together;

o a battery which stores electricity for use when the sun is not shining.

materials produces a tiny electric current. Manufactures have developed very thin flat slices of silicon (the material that sand and glass are made of) so that when they are exposed to light they are able to produce an exploitable current. These 'silicon slices' are known as solar cells and are produced as 10 cm squares. Since the voltage of each cell is around 0.6V, they have to be connected together to produce sufficient electricity to power equipment. A group of 15–30 cells forms a module and one or two modules form a panel.

There are three types of cell: single crystal, polycrystalline and amorphous. All are based on silicon. The single crystal type is the most expensive and has the highest efficiency (12–14%), while the amorphous type has the lowest efficiency (6%) but is the cheapest.

Solar cells produce electricity when placed in sunlight (solar radiation). Therefore to enable electricity to be used at night, the panel has to be used in conjunction with batteries which store the electricity generated by the panel during the day. A simple system suitable for household lighting consists of:

The output from a cell, and hence panel, is dependent upon the intensity of the solar radiation falling on its surface. Halving the intensity of solar radiation reduces the module output by half and lowers the voltage at which the current is produced. This effect can be particularly important during cloudy weather when there may be insufficient voltage to recharge the battery; therefore careful sizing of the system is important.

Solar panels achieve their highest output when the panel is at right angles to the solar radiation falling on its surface. The sun moves in an arc through the sky and its highest position within the arc varies seasonally. This means that the angle of solar radiation falling on the panel also varies. To capture as much solar energy as possible, the panel needs to be adjusted during the day to face the sun. The adjustment can be done manually or automatically. Manual systems allow for the panel orientation to be changed a number of times a day and seasonally. Automatic systems keep the panels orientated to the sun throughout the day. Although they are more efficient than the manual systems, they are more expensive. Manufacturers and suppliers should be able to advise about the orientation for a particular site.

Example 4.3: Estimating output from a PV panel

Detailed sizing of a PV system is outside the scope of this book. However, it is possible to give some guidelines to check manufacturers' claims. For each Wp of rated power, the module should deliver approximately 0.85Wh of electrical energy for each kWh/m²/day of insolation available at the site. In most tropical locations the average insolation is 5kWh/m²/day. Hence a 40Wp module in such a location should deliver 170Wh of energy per day (rated power × insolation × energy delivered per module).

Insolation levels can be obtained from local meteorological stations (see under Resources required). For reliability in estimations, use a figure 20% lower than that quoted by manufacturers.

The time of day at which a panel starts to produce electricity depends upon season and latitude. Panels begin to produce electricity when light of around 10% of noonday sun intensity falls on the panel, and output will continue until light fades in the late afternoon. If shadows fall across the module, the electric output will be reduced. If a single cell is shaded for a long time, it may cause the entire module to fail. Therefore, the correct location of panels is important, with regular checks to see that they are not shaded by trees or crops and that birds have not nested on top of them.

Sizing a solar system

The amount of electricity a solar panel is able to produce depends upon its geographical location because the strength or intensity of sunlight varies from place to place. The closer to the Poles, the more seasonal variations in solar intensity occur. Panels are sold by the power output which is expressed in terms of peak watts (Wp) which is defined as the output at 25°C under a light intensity of 1kW/m². This represents the maximum output under the very best operating conditions. Basically, this means that a system should never be sized on the basis of the maximum output matching the demand

A typical module (0.3 × 0.5 m) containing 36 cells would produce 30–35W DC at 12V in bright sunlight.

It is important to realize that the output also decreases with temperature (a 5 degree Centigrade rise in temperature will reduce the power output by 2.5%). This means that the siting of the panel needs to be carefully chosen. Mounting them on tin roofs can reduce the power output significantly (15% or more). Generally it is recommended that they are mounted on poles and exposed to breezes to keep the surrounding ambient temperature down. The mounting should not be too high since the panels need to be cleaned from time to time. On the other hand, some thought also needs to be given to safe-guarding the panels from theft, since they are easily transportable.

Modules suitable for households and micro-enterprises come in a range of sizes from 5Wp to 60Wp. One of the advantages of solar panels is their flexibility in sizing. Modules can be bought to match the income available, beginning by meeting the most important needs, for example lighting, and adding to the system as and when finances allow.

The battery is the weakest part of the solar energy system, therefore careful selection is needed to ensure reliability and avoid expensive mistakes. Buying the cheapest battery can prove costly. Conversion efficiency of the complete system is 5–10%. Therefore, it is better to try using more energy-efficient appliances, which may cost more but will be cheaper than adding more charging capacity to the system.

Costs

Manufacturers' information needs to be checked carefully to see exactly what is included in the selling price. The costs usually include the panel and the other system components but not the end-use equipment. Automatic tracking systems can add up to 25% to equipment costs. Transport and installation may be extra. Systems suitable for domestic use in the range 30–500Wp cost US$20–30/Wp. In 1995, the cost of a small solar home power system ranged from US$350 up to US$500. Costs of modules are predicted to fall within the next few years. Economies of scale are negligible with solar systems. The running costs in terms of service are not high. However, regular maintenance of the system is required to prolong system life.

Batteries will need to be replaced every 3–5 years and this can form about 30% of the total system costs over the lifetime of the panel. The lifetime of the battery is strongly influenced by the charging and discharging pattern. Too frequent deep discharging of the batteries shortens their life. Battery sizing also significantly influences costs. The greater the variation in radiation levels, the larger is the battery storage requirement. Optimization of the system needs to be carried out to assess whether another back-up might be a better option or if load shedding of non-essential equipment is possible.

Resources required

Photovoltaic systems require high and consistent levels of sunshine. Insolation should be above 5kWh/m²/day for PV systems to be viable. Manufacturers' information needs to be checked for the level of solar insolation the system is designed to operate on. Insolation data, expressed as monthly mean daily solar insolation (kW/m²), is available from local meteorological offices. The insolation figure gives an energy value and should not be confused with mean daily sunshine hours, which gives a time value. If the PV system is to be used for applications requiring a high level of availability, as for example in a rural clinic, the data for the month with the lowest insolation level should be used. However, for most applications, the annual value is generally sufficient.

Batteries are required for using equipment at night and on cloudy days.

A suitable place in direct sunlight, with easy access for cleaning, is needed for mounting the panel. A pole in an open location gives better access than the roofs of buildings.

Users

PV systems are suitable for households, micro-enterprises and community buildings such as schools and health centres where there is no grid electricity and power demands are low. Although individual sets are generally intended for one user, they can be applied at the community level, for example for street lighting (which can provide increased safety) or for water pumping.

There may be cultural objections to women climbing ladders to service panels. However, these objections can be overcome by using panels mounted on poles close to ground level.

The lack of moving parts and a low level of maintenance makes this an attractive system for women who lack experience in dealing with equipment. However, although the daily maintenance requirements are minimal, the need to reorient the panel several times a day can conflict with a woman's other domestic duties.

Reliability, maintenance and safety

The first photovoltaic solar cells were developed in 1954. The technology is technically proven and is commercially available. It is being used in most countries, both developed and developing. Lifetimes for the modules are quoted as over 20 years but more widespread field operating experience is needed to confirm this. Amorphous cells may have significantly shorter lifetimes. Manufacturers usually provide warranties covering 5–7 years.

Maintenance requirements are low and not demanding but need to be carried out systematically. The panels need to be kept free from dust, otherwise their efficiency is reduced. About once a month (possibly more frequently in arid, dusty areas), the glass of the panel needs to be cleaned with a soft cloth (to avoid scratching the surface and reducing the panel efficiency). The panel needs to be checked regularly to ensure that seasonal growth of crops or other biomass is not shading the panel, or that birds have not nested on top of it.

Batteries have generally proved to be the weak link in solar systems, either through the use of car batteries or by not topping up the electrolyte. The terminals need to be cleaned once a month and electrolyte levels should be checked. The cable from the panel to the battery needs to be fused to protect the system against faults (e.g. short circuits) which can lead to fires. The fuse should be at the battery end. The panel should also be earthed to protect the equipment against lightning and people against shocks. The panel frame is connected by heavy gauge earth wires to an earthing rod which is driven into the ground close to the panel.

Expertise needed

Installation may need expert help, particularly with the correct orientation of the panel to achieve optimal output from the cells. The systems require little except systematic maintenance, which can be carried out by a non-technical person after training. However, in household systems it is important to ensure that both male and female members of the household are trained in the use of the system, as women can spend much of the day at home while the men are elsewhere. If the charge controller alarm sounds, women need to know what actions to take.

Environmental impacts

The negative environmental impacts of solar cells are mainly confined to the manufacturing process. There is the possibility of exposure to cadmium if cells based on cadmium catch fire (a very rare event). However, even then the level of exposure is not regarded as dangerous and if this was linked to a roof fire the smoke from the other burning material is likely to be more dangerous. Cadmium should not be allowed to leak into the environment where it can accumulate and enter the human food chain. Therefore, panels which are no longer functioning should be returned to the supplier for recycling.

Conclusion

Solar PV power is suitable for low power demands in households and micro-enterprises, i.e. not exceeding a few kilowatt-hours a day, and where there is

Table 4.8: Advantages and disadvantages of solar (PV) energy

Advantages	Disadvantages
Operation is silent; No pollution during operation; Risk of electric shock is minimal because of the low system voltage; Systems can be sized to meet individual needs and financial resources; Short lead time for installation; No moving parts; Easy to add to as financial resources increase; Running costs are very low; Maintenance costs are very low.	The initial cost is relatively high compared to other options; It produces only relatively small amount of electric energy (not suitable for cooking); It requires batteries for storing energy; Panels need to be adjusted during the day to achieve good efficiency (automatic tracking systems too expensive); Panels need to be kept clean; Panels are fragile and can be broken if stones are thrown etc; Systems have to be imported into most countries.

Case study: Solar PV in Namibia

Ms Helena Martin, the owner of *Bar We Like*, a *cuca* shop near Ondangwa (Owambo district), in Namibia, bought a solar lighting system for 700 Rand in 1985 from a South African student who came to Owambo selling solar kits. Only three other people bought kits at the same time. Ms Martin thinks it was because they did not understand the system and what benefits it could bring. Now many people ask her how to get solar lighting.

Her PV system consists of a 33Wp panel directly charging a Delco 310Ah tractor battery from which she runs three lights and a cassette player for the bar's music. A 9W globe light is used outside and 9W globe and 14W strip lights are used inside from 7 to 10 or 11pm in the *cuca* shop. There is not always enough power to run the outside light. However, Ms Martin is happy with her system as she has incurred little expense since 1985, with only the need to replace bulbs.

Mr and Mrs Andreas Nangolo from Onatsi near Ondangwa own a solar home system consisting of two 33Wp panels, a 250W inverter and a 102Ah battery. The system runs a colour TV, portable black and white TV and four 15W fluorescent lights. The colour TV is the main user of power. In the year and a half since the system was installed, with the exception of the light bulbs which have all had to be replaced, it has performed well. Prior to purchasing the system, they had used candles for lighting. They are slightly disappointed that they are not able to cook or iron with PV electricity.

Source: Solar Energy for Rural Communities: The Case of Namibia by G. Yaron, T. Forbes Irving, and S. Jansson (IT Publications)

no grid connection. PV is not able to meet the levels of power demand for cooking. In sunny remote areas, PV can be economic for loads up to 20kWh/day. The technology is widely available, although it is imported into most developing countries either as completed products or as cells ready for assembly. The selection of the PV system therefore needs to take into account the availability of support by the supplier.

This is a technology which can be attractive to women with little experience of handling equipment, since there are no moving parts and it has low maintenance requirements. There is a risk with household systems that women may be excluded from training in how the system operates yet are left with responsibility for the equipment during the day. Unfortunately, the high initial costs of the system can prove a particular barrier of access to women unless attention is given to their access to credit.

Gasifiers

Introduction

Gasifiers were used extensively at the beginning of the 20th century, but interest in this technology dwindled when cheap petroleum products came on to the market after 1945. However, during the 1970s there was renewed interest in gasification, both in the industrialized and the developing countries, in response to the oil crisis. In developed countries the emphasis was on large-scale applications (for example, in the Swedish and Finnish paper industries). In a number of developing countries, emphasis has been on smaller-scale applications (for example, in Brazil, Mali, Indonesia, India and the Philippines). The gasifier programmes in these countries have mainly been based on locally produced technologies.

During the 1980s many technical difficulties were encountered with gasifiers, which saw a decline in their use. Many of the problems were linked to attempts to use agricultural residues in gasifiers designed for wood, and to a lack of training for operators. However, interest has revived again in the 1990s, most notably in India, which is expected to lead to further improvements in the technology as experience with different fuels increases.

This technology is not suitable for producing electricity for individual households or micro-enterprises. However, it can be used as the basis of a mini-grid for a community.

How gasifiers work

Gasification means burning biomass in a limited supply of oxygen in an enclosed reactor at high temperatures, and so that the combustion process is only partly completed. The result is that the gases which leave the combustion zone are reduced in another part of the gasifier to form a gaseous mixture called producer gas (composed of carbon monoxide, hydrogen and methane, which burn, and carbon dioxide and nitrogen, which do not burn). Also produced are condensable compounds, called tars, and dust.

Producer gas can be used to run a diesel generator to produce electricity. In other words, the producer gas acts as a diesel fuel substitute. However, producer gas does not contain as much energy as diesel fuel and so the diesel engine's maximum output on producer gas is 40–50% less than if it was running on diesel fuel. This has to be kept in mind when sizing the diesel engine to meet the load. Also producer gas does not ignite spontaneously in a diesel engine so some diesel fuel still needs to be used to run the engine.

Figure 4.10: Components of a gasifier system

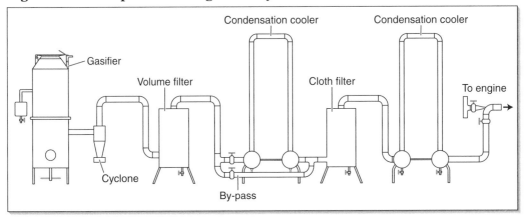

The gas needs to be cooled and cleaned before it enters the engine. Cooling increases the amount of gas entering the engine. Cooling can either be by fins, which dissipate the heat through large metal surface areas, or by water sprays. Dust particles larger than 3 microns (μm) and tars have to be removed to protect the engine and ensure that its lifetime is not reduced significantly. Cyclones and precipitators can remove dust, while filters, made of materials such as coir fibre or fibreglass, can remove the tars. The Figure 4.10 shows the components of a gasifier system.

The diesel engine needs a minor modification to the air intake manifold to enable the producer gas to mix with the intake air. The engine sucks in a specific flow rate of gas/air mixture. Operating the air control valve controls the ratio of gas to air, closing the air flow valve increases the amount of producer gas entering the engine. To stop the engine speed from increasing, the governor on the engine automatically reduces the amount of diesel entering the engine.

Gasifier sizes

A gasifer consists of a circular chamber with a steel outer wall and an inner refractory lining capable of withstanding temperatures of 1000°C. There are inlet ports around the side of the gasifier – just above the grate – which allow for lighting the fuel at start up and for air to enter the combustion zone.

Gasifiers are available in different types, based on the direction of gas flow through the system, and as well as different sizes of power output to suit different energy needs. Those over 100kW are usually used in large-scale industries, for example sawmills. The two gasifiers which are suitable for smaller scale needs are: the down-draught gasifier (which is considered the design with the lowest tar production levels), and the cross-draught gasifier (suitable for power output from less than 10kW). The operation of these systems is shown in the Figure 4.11.

The gasifier unit can be either closed-topped or open-topped. The former has a wider diameter than the latter, and is shorter. The open-topped design is increasingly favoured since it is considered to dry the fuel more effectively and has good tar reducing properties. The open-topped design is also considered to have a lower risk of explosions due to pressure build up.

Figure 4.11: The down-draught and cross-draught gasifier

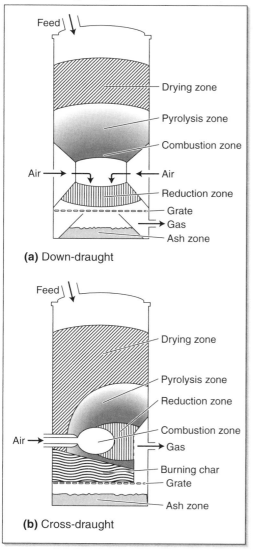

(a) Down-draught

(b) Cross-draught

erator set its output is electrical power. The sizing of equipment can be quoted using the subscripts 'th' (kW_{th}) for the gasifier alone, and 'el' (kW_{el}) for the gasifier/diesel gen-set combination. It is important to check which value a supplier is using to ensure that the correct equipment is purchased since, for the same gasifier, kW_{el} will be lower than kW_{th}.

Costs

A typical down-draught gasifier capable of generating 5–100kW of electricity costs about US$6500. For gasifier gen-sets under $10kW_{el}$, the cleaning equipment can represent a substantial part of the total cost. Operating costs depend on: the fuel used (including collection, transport and preparation), the disposal of waste products such as tar and ash (i.e. transport and trading), and the payment of gasifier operators (since the gasifier cannot be run unattended; a small system needs two operators, one skilled and another semi-skilled per shift).

Diesel fuel should be included in the operating costs as well as lubrication oil for the engine. An engine running on producer gas and diesel (referred to as dual-fuel operation) needs the lubrication oil changing more frequently (approximately twice as often) than when running on diesel oil alone. Maintenance costs of the diesel engine are approximately 10% of capital costs and those for the gasifier are around 5%.

Ash removal takes place through the bottom of the gasifier. This can either be through a removable cap or a water seal which allows the water to wash the ash away on a continuous basis. With the former system, the gasifier operation has to be interrupted to allow for the cap to be taken off and the ash removed.

A gasifier's output is thermal power. However, when it is linked to a diesel gen-

Resources required

Gasifiers can be designed to run on a variety of bio-waste products such as wood waste from sawmills, and agricultural residues of different kinds, especially those with low ash content such as coconut shells. However, each gasifier is designed for a particular type of fuel, which limits its flexibility. For example, gasifiers for wood will not operate on powdery

Example 4.4: Estimating biomass feedstock requirements for a gasifier

A small village of 40 households has an estimated electricity demand of $0.5kW_{el}$ per family to provide lighting, drinking water and to run a grain mill. A group of women in the village decide to explore the possibilities for generating electricity from their own resources. One possibility is to use the residue (stalks and cob) from the maize grown in the village to run a gasifier generator set.

The average load is estimated to be $15kW_{el}$ since the mill will run during the day and the water will be pumped at night. In total the generator is estimated to run for 10 hours per day. Over the year, operation will be for 3600 hours generating 54 000kW of electrical energy.

The quantity of biomass required is estimated by assuming that 1kg of air-dried maize residue will generate 0.7kWh of electricity. Therefore, the amount of maize residue required is approximately 77 tonnes. Their agricultural extension officer tells the women that the amount of residue produced per hectare (ha) is approximately 5.6 tonnes. This means that the land area which would produce sufficient maize residue is around 14ha. Each household allocates on average 0.5ha to maize production, which means that there are 20ha growing maize. This would be sufficient to meet present demand and allow for shortfalls of production or to meet future increases in demand.

This is only the first stage in assessment. The women would then need to consider how the collection could be organized and where the residues would be stored during the year. The maize residue would occupy a volume of over a $1000m^3$. Other important questions are: what are the present uses of the residues and who controls their use? Competing uses, for example as animal fodder, might rule out the residues as an option. If men control the use of the residues within the community they may decide to set other priorities.

---

materials, such as sawdust. Charcoal is generally regarded as the most trouble-free fuel, since it is low in tars, which thus reduces maintenance requirements.

Continuity of fuel supply needs to be ensured. If this is to be bought, a good contract needs to be negotiated, which is an area in which women may lack experience and would need training and support. If the community supplies the fuel, this also needs careful organization to ensure that collection does not add to the women's burden. Fuelling even small gasifiers requires more wood than can be collected from traditional sources. As a planning guide, 1kg of air-dried biomass gives 0.7–0.9kWh of electricity plus 1.4kWh of heat (see Example 4.4). A conversion efficiency of 10 to 30% biomass to electricity can also be used for estimating resource requirements.

The fuel has to be of a standard shape and size and has to be dry (moisture content between 10 and 15%). Control of the moisture content requires a moisture meter and a covered storage area, particularly in the rainy season. The preparation stages consume both time and money. Wood, for example, will need to be chipped and other residues may need to be briquetted (densified).

A diesel gen-set will also be required. Diesel fuel will be needed for operation, around 15–20% of the engine's normal diesel fuel requirements. The engine sucks the gas through the system when it is running. However, at start-up, a fan is needed to draw the gases through the system. This needs an electricity source. Some cooling and cleaning systems require running water for operation.

Users

Generally gasifiers are not used for individual households. Micro-enterprises with sufficient electricity demand could use a small cross-draught gasifier. Gasifiers linked to a diesel generator are appropriate for supplying a community mini-grid. Training of operators is essential for successful gasifier use and care needs to be taken that women are not excluded from access to this training. There is the risk that women could be sidelined into only collecting fuel for the gasifier, which would add to their workload and might conflict with their other tasks.

Reliability, maintenance and safety

Gasifiers can be regarded as a proven technology for operation with wood or charcoal. However, there is limited experience with other feedstocks, which have not been trouble free. Rice husk fuels are particularly problematic and produce large quantities of tar and ash which have to be disposed of. With regular maintenance, lifetimes of gasifier systems are estimated at around 10 000 operating hours.

Locally produced gasifiers are available in only a small number of developing countries; for example, India, China, and Brazil. It is therefore important to check the contract offered by the suppliers, not only for maintenance, but also for troubleshooting during the commissioning stage. A local person with appropriate skills should be available rather than having to wait for expensive outside experts to arrive. The contract needs careful negotiation (which is an area where women may lack expertise and require support).

Gasifiers have fairly strict requirements as to feedstock (fuel) size, moisture content and ash content. Inadequate fuel preparation is a major cause of technical problems. The gas itself must be free from tar and dust particles. This requires regular cleaning of the filter systems and systematic maintenance (for example, one hour three times a week). Depending on the design of the system, operation may have to cease periodically to allow for ash removal which would otherwise lead to blockages in the gas flow.

Gasifiers must not be used in enclosed buildings in case of leakage, since producer gas contains carbon monoxide which can cause asphyxiation at concentrations significantly lower than those found in producer gas. There should be no danger of carbon monoxide leakage during operation since the system operates below atmospheric pressure, which means that gases cannot escape from the system. However, in some gasifier designs pressure can build up in the system due to blockages, and this can lead to explosions. Provision of water seals in the system allows for the safe release of pressure build-up, thus reducing the danger of explosions. Gas continues to be generated for about 20 minutes after the engine has been switched off – so the area around the gasifier should continue to be well ventilated.

In systems with closed lid fuel hoppers, care needs to be taken when opening the lid, that the sudden inlet of air to the system does not lead to flames suddenly leaping out of the top (flashback) causing burns to the operator. Likewise, care should be taken when walking in front of the air inlet ports (which should also not be looked into directly during operation) in case of flashback. The walls of the gasifier become very hot and should not be touched. Children should not be allowed to play near the gasifier.

The diesel engine will need the lubrication oil topping up regularly and a complete change periodically (probably twice as frequently as stated in the manufacturer's intructions, which are for running on diesel only). The fuel filter also needs

---

Case study: Electrification of the Indian village of Hosahalli using a gasifier generator set

The small Indian village of Hosahalli (population about 270) is situated 110km south west of Bangalore in Karnataka state. Prior to 1987 it had no electricity. A steady supply of drinking water was a problem faced by women daily. The women had to walk half a kilometre every time they wanted to fetch water. The water supply was often dry for four months a year. In 1987, Hosahalli became part of a government-integrated energy project to provide electricity by means of a gasifier generator set. One of the conditions of the project was that the village should be willing to provide sufficient land to plant a sustainable wood crop which would be large enough to fuel the gasifier. The villagers were willing and in May 1987, the project was initiated by planting mixed species of trees (including eucalyptus hybrids) on two and half hectares of land.

The land produces 7 tonnes of wood per hectare annually, which provides more than enough fuel for gasification. The gas is used to run a single phase 3.5kW gasifier engine generator set. The state electricity board contributed to the project by providing electricity lines for the 43 houses in the village and a 40W fluorescent and 15W incandescent lamp for each house. In addition six 40W fluorescent lamps were provided for street lighting. The gasifier gen-set has been estimated as saving 0.95 tonnes of kerosene per year in the village.

Electricity became available a year later (May 1988), initially for 4 hours daily; however, 8 months after project implementation, electricity was made available for 6 hours daily. At the end of the first phase of the project, a borehole and pump were installed to pipe water to the village, thus saving the women valuable time and energy.

Source: The Power Guide

---

periodic replacement. The vibration from the engine during operation causes nuts and bolts to work loose. These need to be checked regularly and tightened to safeguard the engine.

Expertise needed

Gasification requires high levels of skill both for installation and maintenance. The associated generator will also require maintenance. A full-time operator who is thoroughly trained to run the system is also necessary, with semi-skilled assistance for fuel preparation and loading. The system supplier should provide this training. The level of operation skills are estimated as higher than those to operate a standard boiler or conventional diesel of comparable size. However, these requirements should not be a barrier to women participating in operating the system.

Environmental impacts

Operators may be exposed to a number of occupational health risks, although these can be reduced or avoided. Carbon monoxide poisoning should be avoided if the gasifier is placed in a well ventilated area. There are risks of explosions and burns but with good operator training these should be minimal. The handling of the

Table 4.9: Summary of advantages and disadvantages of gasifiers

Advantages	Disadvantages
Technology does not require batteries; Unlike solar, wind and hydro power, production is not dependent on weather or seasonal circumstances (provided sufficient dry biomass is available); Short commissioning lead times (6 months).	Not appropriate for individual households or micro-enterprises with small power demands; Does not totally replace diesel fuel requirements; Collection of fuel may add to women's tasks; Regular maintenance/full time well trained operator; In most countries an imported technology; Biomass feedstock requirements are demanding; Problem of tar disposal.

tars produced during gasification could have long-term health implications, as they contain phenols which are regarded as agents which could cause cancer.

The disposal of the tars cleaned from the system needs careful consideration. They should not be discharged into waterways for drinking or disposed of on agricultural land. Waste water treatment systems are possible but add significantly to costs. An alternative is to mix the tars with water and spray on to the biomass to be fed into the gasifier. The tars should then be broken down into producer gas (which would improve the energy efficiency of the system).

Women may regard the health risks associated with the disposal of the tars as unacceptable to their community. They should therefore make sure that they are involved at the planning stage to ensure that they are able to influence system selection.

The source of biomass feedstock needs to be assessed for its environmental impact. Field residues, which normally play a role in the agricultural system, should be avoided since their removal can lead to soil degradation or erosion.

However, if wood lots are grown specifically for fuelling the gasifier, a number of positive environmental benefits can arise. Integration into the farming system can provide windbreaks which reduce soil erosion, lessen the risk and extent of damage from flooding and help to regenerate degraded land. Forested areas also act as watershed protection and help to prevent large-scale erosion in vulnerable areas such as slopes. Careful species selection can also provide a number of other socio-economic benefits.

Conclusion

This technology is more suitable for a community group or for a village than for households or (most) micro-enterprises. The technology has recently undergone a number of developments which have improved the operation on wood but there are still problems with operation on agricultural residues, most notably with rice husk, which produces large amounts of tar. The disposal of the tar in an environmentally benign way is still problematic.

Figure 4.12: Fixed dome biogas digester

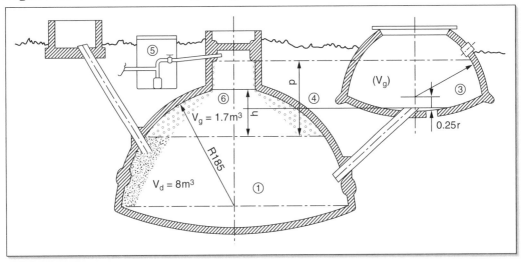

It requires skilled operators and training needs to be provided by the manufacturer/supplier. There is a danger that women might be marginalized in the training and that they may acquire additional tasks in collecting the fuel.

Biogas

Introduction

Biogas is a clean and high-quality fuel in the form of a gas. It contains 60–70% methane, which makes it similar to natural gas and hence it is suitable for any application which can use natural gas or LPG. Biogas is produced through a naturally occurring process, called 'anaerobic digestion' or fermentation, in which biomass material mixed with water is broken down in a leak-proof container (known as a digester) by micro-organisms. It is recognized in many parts of the world as a technology for producing gas which can be used for lighting and cooking. Biogas can also be used for producing electricity by using it to fuel a diesel generator. Although anaerobic digestion is a technology generally associated with rural households in developing countries, it is increasingly being used for waste water treatment in industries. It is therefore particularly appropriate for use with micro-enterprises such as dairies.

How a biogas digester works

There are different types of biogas digesters, one of which is shown in the Figure 4.12.

A fixed dome design consists of an underground digester pit (1), with a dome-shaped cover (4) made of brick or concrete, coated with leakproof cement. The biomass material to be digested is mixed with water (in a ratio of a least 1 part of biomass material to 1 part of water; sometimes more water is needed) and enters the digester via the inlet pipe. The digester is filled up to the bottom level of the expansion chamber (3). After a few days, combustible gas is produced. The number of days (about 10 is normal) depends on the ambient temperature and on the type of material used. Cow dung is quick to start (since it is a good source of the micro-organisms) and it is a good idea, even if other types of biomass are used, to mix some cow dung in with the initial batch of feed material. Under airless conditions, biogas is produced. When the gas valve (5) is closed, biogas collects in the upper part of the digester, which is called the gas storage chamber (6). The gas which collects here displaces part of the slurry (liquid effluent) into the expansion chamber. When the chamber is full, the slurry overflows via the slurry drain into the slurry pit (3) and can be used as high quality manure. When the main valve is opened, the gas leaves the storage section until the slurry levels inside the digester and inside the expansion chamber are balanced. The most common way to operate the digester is to add some feed every day and withdraw some of the slurry (which can be stored until required as a fertilizer or fish food).

The various designs of biogas plants all operate on the same principle but come in different designs and sizes. It is important that a biogas plant should:

o be strong;
o not leak;
o be built with local material in order to reduce its cost;
o be easy to use (in terms of filling) and maintain;
o be reliable.

One of the main disadvantages of biogas digesters is that once installed their output is fixed, so that optimization between present affordable size and likely future increase in demand needs careful balancing.

The most common designs are:

o the floating drum (commonly called the Indian design). It consists of a cylindrical pit in the ground, very similar to a dug water well. The pit is usually lined with bricks. An inverted metal drum, acting as the gas storage chamber, floats in the slurry in the pit;
o the fixed dome (commonly called the Chinese design, as described above);
o the flexible bag (commonly called the Taiwanese design). The original design uses a long cylindrical bag, shaped like a sausage, made of a special type of plastic (which is not destroyed by sunlight). It can either be supported in a trench lined with compacted sand or mud or laid out on the ground.

The biogas is then used to run a diesel generator set. Gas is piped to the engine. The gas contains moisture which tends to condense and has to be removed to prevent blockages. The pipe should dip before it reaches the engine to allow any water condensate to accumulate in a drain from which it can be removed from time to time. The gas also needs to be cleaned of trace amounts of hydrogen sulphide which will cause damage to the metal components of the engine, particularly copper. Removal of hydrogen sulphide can be achieved by passing the biogas through a trap filled with iron oxide (rusty nails or wire wool are good sources) before it enters the engine. From time to time the trap contents can be exposed to air and the iron oxide is regenerated. A small tank, known as a surge tank, can be inserted into the pipeline close to the engine. This ensures a constant pressure of gas entering the engine and allows for smoother operation. The diesel engine needs a minor modification to the air intake manifold to enable the biogas to mix with the intake air. The engine sucks in a specific flow rate of gas/air mixture. Operating the air control valve controls the ratio of gas to air, closing the air flow valve increases the amount of biogas entering the engine. To stop the engine speed increasing, the governor on the engine automatically reduces the amount of diesel entering the engine.

Sizing the system

Sizing a biogas digester needs expert help and is outside the scope of this book. Many of the parameters are site specific, e.g. gas output is dependent upon feedstock composition and ambient temperature. However, a few guidelines can be given. Approximately $0.75m^3$ of biogas is required to generate 1kWh of electricity. A fixed dome design produces between 0.15 and $0.3m^3$ of gas a day per cubic metre of digester, while a floating dome design produces between 0.3 and $0.6m^3$ of gas a day per cubic metre of digester. So, for example, if a micro-enterprise with a daily electricity demand of 5kWh was considering installing a fixed dome digester then the volume of the digester would need to be at least $20m^3$. The quantity of gas needed to generate the electricity is produced by the dung from at least ten cows (the dung from one cow produces around 360 litres of biogas per day).

Costs

The cost is highly site specific and depends on material and labour costs, location, and the type selected. For example, in Kenya a $10m^3$ fixed dome plant cost US$500 and a similar size cost US$1100 in Burkina Faso, in the same year. Depending on the design, the required investment can be high. For example, a fixed dome plant can cost between US$50 and US$150/m^3, while a float steel drum can cost between US$100 and US$200/m^3 (and is highly sensitive to the local cost of steel). Transportation of the material to construct the digester can also add to costs, for example, importation of the

plastic bag or transporting the metal dome.

The cost of the piping, engine and generator needs to be added to these costs. These additional costs may prove unacceptable to individual households where the requirement is for only a few kilowatts to run a couple of lights and a TV and cheaper alternatives exist. Most households would generally only consider investing in a biogas digester for meeting cooking needs and gas lighting, thereby avoiding the extra costs of the diesel genset. Micro-enterprises and communities should find it easier to absorb these extra costs.

The running costs are not easy to define. They include unpaid work such as the labour needed to collect the biomass feed and fetch water in order to feed the digester every day. The time this takes could be significant, particularly if the materials have to be collected from some distance away (experience shows that water collection has been a particular problem, especially when head loaded). This is a task which has generally been undertaken by women and can add significantly to their workload.

Maintenance costs need to be taken into account, both for the digester and for the diesel generator. The maintenance costs for the floating dome are higher than for other designs, since this involves painting the drum once a year to ensure long life. The replacement costs of the steel drum are around one-third of the cost of the new plant. Bags can last up to 10 years but they need to be well protected from sharp implements and animal claws.

A small amount of diesel fuel is needed to start the generator; however, the cost is lower than when the engine runs on diesel alone. However, dual-fuel operation (biogas and diesel) requires the lubrication oil to be changed more frequently (approximately twice as often) than when running on diesel oil alone.

Resources required

The type of material and the quantity available are important factors in deciding upon the size of digester needed and how much biogas (and therefore electricity) will be obtained. Any organic material can be converted into biogas. The rate at which biogas is produced and the amount varies with the type of feed material and temperature. For example, woody materials such as straw are very difficult to digest, while cow dung digests easily. Some material may be difficult to collect; for example, dung from animals not usually kept in stalls, such as sheep. For other materials, pre-treatment may be needed, for example, water hyacinth (a water weed) needs to be chopped before feeding into the digester. It is also possible to link latrines to feed directly into the digester. This is a very good method of treating human excreta (night-soil) and can do a lot to reduce the spread of many common diseases (e.g. cholera). The use of electricity generated from the biogas does not appear to have met with cultural resistance.

The waste water from a number of industrial processes connected with agricultural products processing, such as tanneries, dairies and slaughterhouses, can also be treated anaerobically. These industries can either be micro-enterprises or they can be on a larger scale within a community. The disposal of these wastes often has negative impacts on the environment, causing oxygen depletion if discharged into water and affecting soil fertility if discharged on to the land. Anaerobic wastewater treatment is cheaper than many of the conventional aerobic methods and can reduce pollution by 95%. In addition, because the material is enclosed in a digester, the smell is much less than that from one of the most common treatment processes, lagooning. Anaerobic digestion also offers the possibility of providing a useful energy by-product which can be used in the industry itself or can be sold to the surrounding community. For the treatment of large volumes of waste, a different digester design from those used in households is needed. Women can lobby local industries to install the technology to bring environmental improvements to their communities and possibly also electricity to their homes.

Water is an important input which is often overlooked. The quantities can be significant. As a guideline, for most household feedstocks, the minimum water requirement can be the same volume as the amount of biomass feedstock. For example, the figures given in the section on sizing the system were for a digester fed with the dung from ten cows. Each cow produces around 10kg of manure a day. Therefore 100kg of dung would need to be mixed daily with 100 litres of water (at least). If this water has to be head-loaded this can significantly add to women's workload.

The (air) temperature is also important. Biogas production is not economic when the average temperature is below 20°C. This rules it out as an appropriate technology in many high altitude areas or in places where there are distinct seasonal temperature differences.

The diesel engine needs a battery to start and about 15–20% of its normal diesel fuel input to burn the biogas inside the engine. Engine lubrication oil is needed at twice the rate as when running on diesel fuel alone.

Users

Biogas plants come in a variety of sizes and can be coupled with generators of different sizes. They can therefore be appropriate both for individual households and micro-enterprises or for community use. There is widespread experience with biogas digesters in developing countries and women have generally played an active part in the daily maintenance of the plants. This type of experience of handling a new technology can be built on to enable them to operate the diesel generator. There appears to have been little attempt to involve women in the construction of plants.

Reliability, maintenance and safety

Biogas has been used successfully in many developing countries. China, Nepal, Taiwan and India use biogas on a large scale. Some Chinese plants have lasted for 50 years. With the exception of the plastic bag, which is often imported, the technology is constructed locally. This means that local expertise is readily available. Biogas digesters in the past have been disseminated through programmes which have not always been successful, probably due to poor 'after-sales' service. However, there are a number of commercial companies now appearing and offering a more comprehensive service.

Biogas digesters should have few problems if well made and operated correctly. Construction faults (poor quality materials and badly trained constructors) are the main cause of problems and the construction needs to be checked before commissioning. Sudden changes in temperature, feed rate and feed composition can cause a reduction in gas production but after a few days the system should recover by itself. Antibiotics (which can be excreted in human and animal urine), chemical sprays and disinfectants should be prevented from entering the digester,

since they can kill the micro-organisms producing the biogas.

The digester itself does not require regular expert maintenance or servicing and in general the owner can do most of the work. New feedstock and water have to be collected daily and mixed to add to the digester. Some designs require that the complete digester contents be mixed once a day. The gas pressure needs to be checked. The liquid slurry has to be emptied and taken to the fields or for drying (again this can be an additional task for women). Inlet and outlet pipes need to be checked regularly for blockages, which affect gas production. The water trap has to be inspected weekly and emptied. Gas valves should be oiled monthly to keep them from getting stiff. They should also be tested for leaks, using soapy water solution to detect bubbles caused by any escaping gas.

The steel drum should be painted once a year to prevent it from rusting. The fixed dome or bag plants do not need painting. In this regard the fixed dome and bag plants have lower yearly running costs. Scum formation on the surface of the digesting material should be checked annually and removed if necessary. All systems need to be stopped every few years so that accumulated debris, such as stones, can be removed. First the pit must be emptied and (as a safety measure) must remain empty for at least 24 hours before entering the pit to start the repairs (biogas in the confined space of the digester can cause suffocation). No one should enter the pit without having another person assisting on top. The person entering the pit should have a rope tied around their middle, held by the assistant, ready to pull them out if they show signs of breathing difficulties. In order to avoid explosions, there should be no naked flames or lighted cigarettes in or around the digester while this process is being carried out.

Table 4.10: Advantages and disadvantages of biogas

Advantages	Disadvantages
Effective use of dung providing fertilizer and electricity; Can bring hygiene and sanitation improvements.	Collection of the feedstock and feeding the plant can be time consuming; Size of digester is fixed when it is installed, which may restrict its ability to meet increases in demand; It does not produce electricity directly, but needs a generator.

Gas or water should not be allowed to leak from the digester. The smell of bad eggs indicates leaks in the gas storage and a drop in the slurry level indicates a water leak. Any leaks must be carefully repaired, which will require emptying the digester following the safety procedures given in the previous paragraph.

The diesel engine will need the lubrication oil topping up regularly and a complete change from time to time (probably twice as frequently as stated in the manufacturer's instructions, which are for running on diesel only). The fuel filter also needs to be replaced periodically. The vibration from the engine during operation causes nuts and bolts to work loose. These need to be checked regularly and tightened to safeguard the engine.

Expertise needed

A biogas engineer is required to size the biogas unit correctly. Skilled builders are required to build and install the digester. They should ensure that the foundation and wall are pounded firm, the stones are properly cleaned before use and that the cement or sand used does not contain dirt particles and is suitable for making a watertight layer. Operation of the digester requires no special skills, although some initial training is required on the daily feeding requirements, mixing of contents and slurry handling.

Installing the generator requires specialist skills. Technical expertise would be required for major maintenance and repair of the generator, although weekly servicing and simple repairs can be done after training.

This is a technology which women in developing countries may already be familiar with and will often have responsibility for its daily maintenance. They do not appear to be included in training schemes for building and running the electricity generation aspects. Since men need to receive training to carry out these activities, women should also be offered the opportunity to extend their skills and income generating opportunities.

Environmental impacts

Biogas offers many opportunities for positive environmental impacts. Even the use of agricultural residues as a feedstock removes them only temporarily from the system and many users claim that the fertilizer quality of the digested slurry is better than the material that has not passed through the digester. Where industrial wastes are used, biogas production offers the prospect of significant reductions in the pollution of waterways and land. Smell is also eliminated. If human waste is also included in the feedstock, control of many common tropical diseases can be an added benefit.

Case study: Biogas in Senegal

CERSCOR, an NGO from Senegal involved in the dissemination of renewable energy technologies, has been involved with a biogas project for the women of Tambama village. Tambama is a poor village of 136 inhabitants, of whom 66 are women. The village also has a large herd of around 350 cows. This resource is a mixed blessing: on the one hand the cows provide the women with one of their few sources of income, the sale of milk, while on the other hand they create a lot of pollution with their dung.

Contact was made with the villagers through one of CERSCOR's technicians who originates from Tambama. The technician considered that biogas might be an interesting option for helping the villagers to improve their living standards. There would certainly be sufficient dung and water from the wells, the two essential inputs in biogas production.

Participation by the villagers in the project was given a high priority by CERSCOR. During a sensitization phase they were asked to identify their problems. The drudgery of firewood collection for women and the lack of lighting, especially for the mosque, were singled out as the most pressing problems. The villagers indicated their willingness to participate in a project and the beneficiaries of the stoves and lamps were identified.

Two 8m^3 digesters were built using local materials (stones, wood and straw) and local labour. Building the digesters was difficult since the site chosen was on rock. Unfortunately some of the masonry work had to be re-done several times during the rainy season. The costs were FG248 000 and FG384 000 for labour. These were paid for by the Institute of Energy of French Speaking Countries (IEPF). Organization of the work was by a management committee. The women of the village staked a place on the committee, which resulted in four young women learning to read and receiving technical training in how to deal with the breakdowns of the lamps and stoves.

At the beginning of 1997, the mosque and 12 families had lighting and four kitchens also had gas for cooking. This has meant a saving of FG700 per week on kerosene for lighting. Less time spent on fuel wood collection has meant more time for other activities. The village is also cleaner.

Villagers are now strongly motivated to tackle their environmental problems and to take over running the project themselves. A feeling of self-confidence has been generated and villagers are exploring the use of the effluent from the digesters, as well as considering building a school and starting other income-generating activities.

Source: Billy A. Sow, AGUIPER, Guineé

Conclusion

Biogas is suitable for individual house-holds (although the economics of electricity might be unfeasible at this level), micro-enterprises and community systems. It is a technology indigenous in many developing countries with which women have been involved. However, the level of involvement appears mainly linked to feedstock and water collection, and dealing with the slurry. This has added, sometimes considerably, to their daily workload and the collection of water, in particular, has been the cause of digesters being abandoned. More attention needs to be given to getting women involved in other aspects of the biogas electricity generating system.

Steam

Introduction

The ability of steam power plants to use locally available solid and residual fuels, has prompted a growing interest in small-scale plants. Steam engine generating sets can be used to provide electricity in remote areas of developing countries where conventional fuels are expensive or unavailable, and an appropriate biomass supply is available, either dedicated forestry plantations or residues from an agro-processing industry.

Steam is mostly used in big industries and at present less widely used in the small-scale sector. The use of steam engine generating sets to provide up to 100kW of electricity will be discussed.

How steam power works

The steam system consists of three parts: the furnace, the pressure vessel and the steam engine.

The furnace is where the fuel is burnt. There are different furnace designs which differ with the type of fuel. They may use natural draught or forced draught (using a fan) to feed air into the combustion zone.

The heat generated in the furnace is transferred to the water in the pressure vessel. The construction of the unit determines the maximum safe pressure that can be allowed and a safety valve lets off excess pressure.

The heat content of the water is increased and most of the water turns into vapour (steam). The steam can be used to run an engine either to generate electricity or to produce both heat and electricity. The latter is known as combined heat and power (CHP) or co-generation and is used extensively in sugar and other agro-processing industries.

A steam engine works in a similar fashion to a car engine: a piston is pushed down by hot gases expanding. However, in this case it is steam which is expanding, not the combustion products or petrol or diesel. The piston expansion rotates a shaft which generates the electricity. The quantity of power produced depends on the amount of expansion. The greater the expansion, the more power. In some systems a condenser is used to increase the power output. Expansion causes only part of the steam to turn back to water. The remaining steam leaves the engine as exhaust.

Normally the furnace and the pressure vessel are found together in a single unit known as the boiler. There are three types of boilers which can be used: shell, fire-tube and water-tube. The shell boiler is the simplest, with the heat source in direct contact with a closed vessel containing the water used to generate steam. The other two types have largely replaced the shell boiler. The fire-tube boiler increases the surface area contact between the hot gases from the fire and the water,

Figure 4.13: Layout of a steam engine set-up

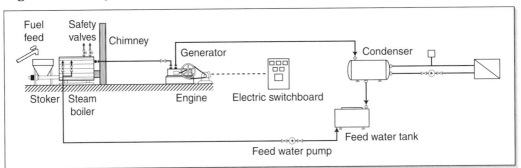

to give increased efficiency, by passing the gases through a series of tubes surrounded by water. There are many possible tube arrangements, in horizontal, vertical or inclined positions. Fire-tubes have a small capacity and can be used only with low pressure steam. Water-tube boilers work on the reverse principle to fire tube-boilers, with the flue gases passing over the outside of the tubes containing the water to be heated. They can be used at higher pressures than fire-tube boilers and have larger capacities. Again, a number of different types exist based on tube arrangements.

The choice of boiler system is influenced by the availability of water. The simplest systems, usually up to 100kW, operate on an open cycle which requires a continuous supply of clean water for the boiler. If the water is 'hard' (that is, it contains a lot of dissolved minerals and salts, recognized by the difficulty in creating bubbles with soap and water) then this must be treated with chemicals to prevent deposits building up on heat exchanger surfaces, which would lead to a reduced efficiency. Chemical treatment also reduces corrosion. Water treatment can add significantly to operating costs. Although open cycle systems are easy to operate, the efficiencies are less than 5%, which influences the quantities of biomass required. Much lower water demands are found with closed cycle systems. Here, the exhaust steam is condensed after it leaves the engine or turbine and the water can be recycled to the boiler. Higher efficiencies (up to 18%) can be obtained from a closed cycle system. The smallest available systems of this type are 200kW. Other cycle variations exist with intermediate efficiencies.

Sizes available

A variety of designs are available in the 5kW–100kW range and manufacturers are found in many developing countries; for example, India, China and Brazil.

Costs

The capital cost of a typical steam generator would be several times that of an equivalent diesel engine set, mainly due to the cost of the boiler and furnace. In 1994, a simple system of 200kW was quoted at US\$135/kW$_{el}$ for the engine plus US\$500/kW for the boiler and auxiliaries, whereas a 200kW diesel engine is approximately US\$50/kW. However, the high cost of the steam system needs to be offset against their lifetime and the fact that steam generators have lower running costs. A well-maintained diesel engine has an expected lifetime of 5–10 years. A steam engine has a minimum lifetime of 20 years, and some have been in operation in developing countries for more than 50 years.

The capital costs are also influenced by the other system components, such as preparation of the biomass; e.g. chipping, storage of the feedstock, transport from storage to furnace, automatic control systems and handling and disposal of ash. Many of these processes can be automated; however, this adds to the costs.

Steam systems have low running costs if using agro-processing residues from an adjoining system, but because of the installation costs they are unlikely to be competitive with diesel engines for small users, unless diesel fuel is very expensive or difficult to obtain. If wood is being grown specifically to fuel the steam system, these costs will also have to be taken into account.

Operating costs include the chemicals for water treatment, as well as the biomass feedstock if the system is not using agro-processing waste.

Resources required

Steam power can be produced from wood and from agricultural residues such as straw, bagasse (sugar cane waste), coconut shells or rice husks. Many of these fuels are cheap in comparison with diesel and might be creating environmental problems with their disposal. To estimate the quantities of biomass required, a calculation similar to that for gasifiers (in Example 4.4) needs to be carried out. It is also important to ensure that there is continuity of feedstock supply, which may require adequate storage space.

Clean water is required for boiler operation. If the water is hard, chemicals for treatment will be needed. Some furnaces require a fan, and hence an electricity supply, to provide sufficient combustion air. Systems using automatic transport for feed and ash disposal will also need electricity.

Users

Steam engines are not suitable for providing electricity to individual households although they may in certain circumstances be suitable for micro-enterprises (those dealing in agro-processing with a process heat requirement for example) or for whole communities. Many large-scale agro-processing industries are located in rural areas and are already using steam to generate electricity for their own use. They often have surplus capacity; that is, they can generate more electricity than they need. However, at present, legislation usually prevents them from selling this electricity to local potential consumers.

Reliability, maintenance and safety

The technology is well established with considerable operating experience throughout the world. Steam engines have a high degree of reliability. However, they have generally been designed for large users. There is a real need for the development of modern small-scale (5–100kW) steam engines suitable for electricity generation in remote areas. Most of the recent developments in steam technology have been on a large scale and with turbines.

Maintenance requirements are that the boiler/heat exchanger tubes are kept clean; the frequency of cleaning depends upon the ash content of the fuel. The ash needs to be removed regularly so that the air flow within the system is not impeded,

Table 4.11: Advantages and disadvantages of steam power

Advantages	Disadvantages
It is a mature technology, with considerable operating experience in developing countries; It is able to utilize the waste from many agro-processing industries which would otherwise cause disposal problems; Low nitrogen oxide emissions when using biomass compared with coal; Dedicated woodlots can help improve soil stability and protect watersheds.	Small-scale systems for households and most micro-enterprises are not available; High costs; High skills level to operate.

reducing the energy conversion efficiency. In simple systems, this requires reduced firing, and hence power output, for an hour a day to enable manual removal of the ash.

Safety is a major consideration with steam engines because of the high pressures of steam used. Explosions could cause serious injuries. As a result, many countries have strict regulations regarding the operation of steam engines, for example, annual safety checks by certified engineers. Fortunately, the number of accidents due to explosions is relatively small.

Expertise needed

Highly qualified engineers are required to install and certify that the engines are operated properly. Thorough training by the equipment supplier is required for the efficient operation of steam engines, for example regulation of combustion air.

Environmental impacts

The environmental impacts of the steam system are both positive and negative. If biomass residues which are causing disposal problems are used as feedstock, there is a positive environmental impact. If wood lots are grown specifically for fuelling the system, positive environmen-

tal benefits can arise. Integration into the farming system can provide wind breaks which reduce soil erosion, lessen the risk and extent of damage from flooding and help to regenerate degraded land. Forested areas also act as watershed protection and help to prevent large-scale erosion in vulnerable sites such as slopes. Careful species selection can also provide other socio-economic benefits.

Ash formed during combustion can leave with the exhaust gases and be dispersed in the surrounding area. There are mechanisms for preventing this happening, which add to the costs. Ash from the furnace needs to be disposed of. The quantities from a small steam system should not be significant and will depend on the type of biomass. The ash can be used for filling in holes in roads, for making cement and has some fertilizer value. There are insignificant nitrogen oxide emissions from biomass combustion systems, which hence do not cause acid rain.

Water is only temporarily removed from waterways so this should not affect aquatic life. The water discharged from large systems can increase the temperature of the water close to the discharge point. Even if this is only by one or two degrees centigrade this can damage aquatic life. Although this is not likely to be a problem with systems under 100kW, it is wise to monitor any discharges. Cooling plants are available, although this adds to costs.

Conclusion

A steam system to provide electricity to remote areas where there is no grid electricity offers a reliable technology, but with high investment costs. It is not available at the scale suitable for use in individual households and most micro-enterprises; however, it can feed into a mini-grid for community consumption.

Batteries: an option for stand-alone generation of electricity or a storage facility

---

Batteries come in different forms, but they all work on the same principle. A battery is a store of chemical energy. It consists of a cell or a group of cells, with two metal terminals. One is positive (marked with +) and one is negative (marked with −). Joining those two terminals with a metal wire via a suitable piece of equipment, such as a radio, makes an electric circuit. Switching on the equipment causes the chemical energy to be converted into electrical energy which flows along the wire. This process is known as discharging and current will continue to flow until a point is reached where no more electricity is generated, and the battery is said to be flat. Some batteries can be used only once (such as the common dry cell type used to power radios), while others can be recharged many times. (Recharging converts electrical energy to chemical energy.) Rechargeable batteries are called secondary batteries or accumulators. Batteries lose charge through leakage if they are left unused; the rate at which this happens depends upon the battery type. Older batteries lose charge more quickly than new ones.

Batteries produce DC electricity. They therefore have to be used with an inverter to convert the current to AC, or appliances capable of being used with DC supply have to be used. Similarly batteries cannot be recharged directly with an AC supply but need a rectifier (or battery charger) to convert the current to DC.

Battery size

Batteries come in a wide range of sizes and manufacturers generally describe their products by three factors: storage capacity, cycle life and depth of discharge.

Storage capacity
Amount of charge the battery can hold, usually expressed in ampere-hours (Ah). For example, a battery of 100Ah would under standard operating conditions give a 5 amp current for 20 hours. Battery suppliers frequently use 20 hours as a basis for data on storage capacity. However, this is a guide only since the capacity changes with the age of the battery, condition, temperature, and rate at which power is drawn from it. For example, a battery at 0°C will hold about 20% less charge than the same battery at 40°C.

Depth of discharge (DOD)
The extent to which a battery is capable of being discharged without damage under normal operation. DOD is expressed as a percentage of the rated capacity, and typically varies from 50 to 100% depending upon the type of battery. In this context batteries come in two forms: *deep discharge* (such as NiCad which can be discharged to 40% regularly) and *shallow discharge* (such as car batteries which can be discharged to only 80% of their rated capacity). DOD is significantly influenced

by temperature, and decreases as temperatures falls. Frequent deep discharges (to around 50% of rated capacity) shorten the battery's lifetime.

Cycle life

A battery can be charged and discharged (a cycle) and the number of times this process can be repeated is the cycle life. The actual time varies with the different types of battery, also for the same battery with the extent to which it is discharged. For example, BP Solar P series batteries can be discharged by 10% DOD over 7200 cycles, 50% DOD over 3000 cycles and 75% DOD over 1500 cycles.

Sizing a battery system

If a battery is too small for the system, it will sometimes be completely discharged and sometimes overcharged. This will damage the battery. On the other hand, too large a battery system is a waste of money. Therefore, there needs to be good matching between energy supply and demand. The modularity of batteries makes it easy to add to the system to match any future growth in demand.

The factors that need to be taken into account when calculating the storage capacity for a system incorporating batteries are: the total daily system charge requirements in Ampere-hours (Ah); the number of storage days required; and the maximum daily DOD.

The required battery size can be calculated as follows:

A worked example can be found in Example 4.5.

It is possible to alter the voltage and storage capacity of the system by connecting a number of batteries together. There are two ways in which the connections can be organized (see Figure 4.14). The components in the system can be joined *in series* in which they are wired up end to end in a continuous chain. In terms of electrical output, if two batteries of the same voltage are connected in series, the voltage increases but the current remains the same. So if two batteries of the same voltage and storage capacity are connected in series, the voltage doubles while the storage capacity remains the same. The other method is to connect the batteries *in parallel*, which in terms of electrical output, if two batteries of the same voltage are connected in parallel, the voltage remains the same but the current increases. So if two batteries of the same voltage and storage capacity are connected in parallel, the voltage remains the same while the storage capacity doubles.

Costs

Battery costs vary with quality and type of electrolyte. Cost comparisons have to be made on a watt-hour (Wh) or rated ampere-hour (Ah) × voltage basis. In the mid-1990s, lead-acid deep cycle, liquid-electrolyte batteries in the USA cost around US$1.10–1.60 per rated Ah for good quality 12V models. For gel-

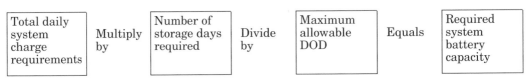

| Total daily system charge requirements | Multiply by | Number of storage days required | Divide by | Maximum allowable DOD | Equals | Required system battery capacity |

Source: Adapted from *Small Solar Electric Systems for Africa*, Mark Hankins 1995

Example 4.5: Sizing battery requirements

A family's daily electrical energy requirement is 240Wh a day. Their appliances can all be run off a 12V supply and they are in use for 6 hours per day. The first step in estimating their battery storage requirements is to calculate the household's daily charge requirements in Amp-hours (Ah) given by:

$$\frac{\text{Energy}}{\text{Voltage}} \ = \ \frac{240}{12} \ = \ 20\text{Ah}$$

Therefore the battery must have a capacity to meet this daily requirement.

However, it is not sufficient to cover only the night-time needs but also the days when there is insufficient sun to charge the battery. The area where the family lives experiences cloudy periods lasting not more than five days. The battery system must have a capacity that is sufficient for at least 5 days.

The maximum allowable depth of discharge of the batteries available is 40%. Therefore the system size can be calculated from:

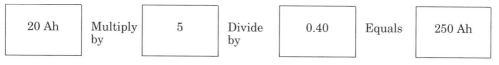

| 20 Ah | Multiply by | 5 | Divide by | 0.40 | Equals | 250 Ah |

Although the family uses only 20Ah a day, it needs a battery system with a capacity of at least 250Ah. A smaller battery would give fewer days security of supply (and might be subject to too frequent complete discharge, thereby shortening its life). A larger battery would be more expensive.

electrolyte batteries the price was US$1.75 per rated Ah for 12V models. Added to the battery costs are those for cables and wiring, as well as the need for a storage room or shed.

Reliability, maintenance and safety

Batteries are an established technology and developments are continually appearing on the market which reduce costs and adapt batteries for use with renewable energy sources. If a battery is well maintained and not over-discharged it should give reliable service.

Batteries should be stored in a cool, dry and well-ventilated place (to avoid explosions) where there is no chance of them being knocked over. The electrolyte level

Figure 4.14: Parallel and series electrical connections

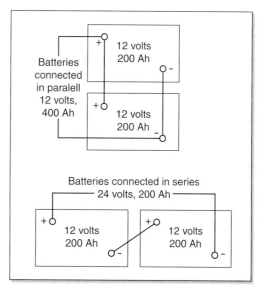

needs to be checked regularly and the electrodes need to be kept clean and free from corrosion.

Batteries are not dangerous to use if a few simple safety procedures are observed. This may be a technology that women have had contact with due to their wide availability. However, knowing what a battery looks like is not the same as familiarity with handling the technology. If the charge controller alarm sounds it is important to know what to do. Therefore, it is important to ensure that women as well as men are included in any training or demonstration for household RPS systems.

All loads should be disconnected and mains switches should be off before attempting to disconnect battery cables or leads. Batteries should not be touched with wet hands and the use of rubber gloves and tools with rubber coated handles is recommended. Some batteries contain dilute sulphuric acid, which should not come into contact with eyes, skin, clothing or other materials. If physical contact is made between the skin and the electrolyte, the affected area should be washed (preferably with running water) and a solution of baking soda mixed with water (not petroleum jelly) applied covered with a dry cloth. If there is acid contact with the eyes, splash water in the eyes for 5 minutes, apply two drops of castor oil (if available) to the eye and cover with a compress dipped in a solution of salt water. Medical attention should be obtained immediately. It is important to train women in this simple first aid procedure because their daily activities frequently keep them in close proximity to the house and they are most likely to be on hand in the event of an accident.

RPS and batteries

The RPS discussed in this book vary in their requirements for batteries as back-up storage. Conversion systems which are usually used in conjunction with battery storage are solar power and wind power, since these resources are subject to interruptions. Technologies which may also use batteries include diesel generators (for use at night to reduce noise) and micro-hydro systems (seasonal variations in flow). Technologies which do not usually use batteries are biogas, gasifiers and steam power.

Batteries which are operating in a circuit which also include other RPS are subject to damage due to over-charging, deep discharge and fluctuations in voltage levels. Batteries can be protected from this type of damage by the inclusion of a charge controller (or voltage regulator) in the circuit, which monitors the state of charge of the battery and responds accordingly. It is not essential to use a charge controller, which can be expensive; however, they could repay the investment by reducing (although not totally eliminating) the amount of attention the system needs and protecting the equipment from damage. It is also possible to include a low-voltage alarm which informs the user (through a visual or audible signal) if the system is malfunctioning. The battery should then be disconnected temporarily from the system while it is recharged. Some users keep two batteries, with one in use while the other is on charge. This, of course, adds to the system costs.

Battery types for use with RPS

The two most common sorts of batteries associated with power generating systems are the lead-acid and nickel cadmium (known as Ni-Cad) batteries. They work on the same principle but are constructed differently.

The lead-acid storage battery (like those used in motor vehicles) consists of a number of cells. Each cell contains two separate plates, one positive and one negative, immersed in an acid solution. The storage capacity of the battery depends on the size, thickness and number of plates. Most common batteries have cells with a voltage of 2.1V when fully charged and the standard size car battery is 12V. Other sizes (for example 6, 24 and 48V) are also available. One of the disadvantages of standard lead-acid batteries is the need for the electrolyte to be topped up from time to time. This is not always practical in remote locations and new types have begun to appear on the market which require less maintenance, such as sealed batteries, although these are more expensive than the standard lead-acid battery.

The most familiar form of Ni-Cad battery is the small rechargeable type used for radios and torches which are known as dry cells since they have no liquid electrolyte. A fully charged Ni-Cad cell has a voltage of about 1.3V. Larger Ni-Cad batteries have also been developed with a liquid electrolyte for use with wind turbines. These require less frequent topping up of the electrolyte than lead-acid batteries operating under similar conditions, which in some applications might help to offset their higher cost.

The voltage, current and storage capabilities of the system can be increased by connecting a number of batteries (which should always be of the same type and age) to form a battery bank. Small batteries (for example, 12V and 100Ah) are easy to transport and hence are susceptible to theft. They should be stored in a secure place which, for safety reasons, should have good ventilation.

The choice of battery needs careful attention since it can have a significant effect on both capital and running costs. Battery costs can form a substantial part of the total system costs. Batteries are

Figure 4.15: Sealed lead-acid storage battery

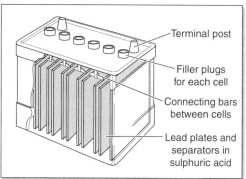

Terminal post

Filler plugs for each cell

Connecting bars between cells

Lead plates and separators in sulphuric acid

Figure 4.16: Ni-Cad battery

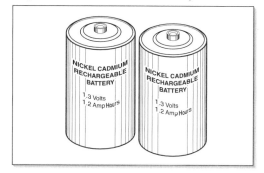

NICKEL CADMIUM RECHARGEABLE BATTERY

1.3 Volts
1.2 AmpHours

NICKEL CADMIUM RECHARGEABLE BATTERY

1.3 Volts
1.2 AmpHours

the weak link in the RPS. Good batteries are expensive and there is the temptation to buy car batteries because they are cheap. However, car batteries are not designed for the type of patterns of charge and discharge that are frequently encountered in RPS, which rapidly shortens their life. They therefore need more frequent replacement and are a false economy compared with a battery designed specifically for an RPS system.

Reliability, maintenance and safety

Batteries do not last forever and so replacement has to be planned for. Following the manufacturer's instructions for the simple maintenance requirements of

Table 4.12. Advantages and disadvantages of Ni-Cad and lead-acid batteries

Type	Advantages	Disadvantages
Ni-Cad	Strong and have a long life; Capable of remaining at low levels of charge for a long time; Remain charged for a long time; Not damaged by being completely discharged; Operate in wide temperature range.	Expensive (5 to 6 times cost of lead-acid).
Lead-acid	Relatively cheap; Readily available.	Contain corrosive acid, which can give nasty burns and damage material; Liable to damage when completely discharged; Need regular maintenance.

keeping the contacts clean and topping up the electrolyte (where appropriate) as required will ensure that the battery performs well and also achieves its expected lifetime. The state of charge should be checked regularly.

In general, battery life depends on the number of times a battery is charged. It is also influenced by other factors, such as storage temperature. Over-charging (that is, continuing to charge the battery after it has reached its 100% charge level) on a regular basis can also lead to damage. A battery's ability to be recharged gradually deteriorates over time. When this is down to 20% of its rated capacity, the battery must be replaced. Battery life for stand-alone systems can be expected to be between 3 and 7 years.

Environmental impacts

Batteries have no environmental impacts during normal operation and they are quiet when in use. If recharging is carried out too quickly, hydrogen gas can be produced which, in poorly ventilated conditions, can lead to explosions. The most significant environmental impact from batteries is in their disposal. Batteries

are made from chemicals which can cause burns (sulphuric acid) or long-term damage to health (cadmium). They should be returned to the supplier or a recycling centre for safe disposal. Children should not be allowed to play with them or allowed to dismantle them.

Costs of small-scale energy systems

It is impossible to give general costs of electricity production from individual systems or stand-alone systems for small grids since there are too many site-specific factors which need to be taken into account. Figure 4-17 gives an overview of examples of electricity costs (in US$/kWh) from a number of technologies under a set of specific conditions and therefore they are indicative only. Biomass was not included because it was considered that the costs were far too site specific. Capital costs are influenced by interest rates and the length of any loan repayment (longer loan repayment periods, at the same rate of interest, give more favourable costs for capital-

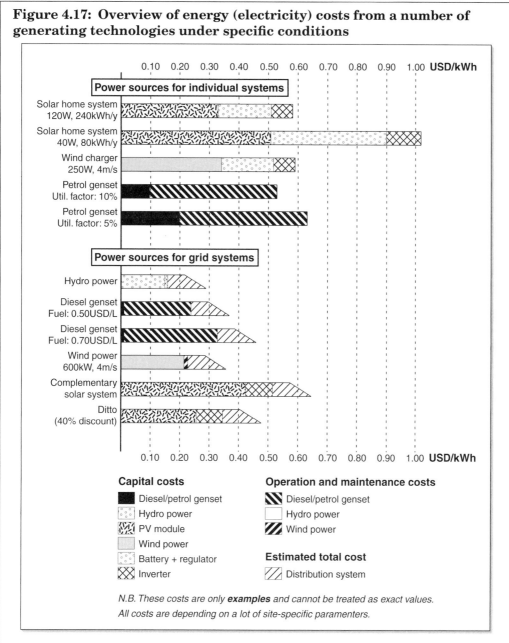

Figure 4.17: Overview of energy (electricity) costs from a number of generating technologies under specific conditions

N.B. These costs are only *examples* and cannot be treated as exact values.

All costs are depending on a lot of site-specific parameters.

Assumptions:
○ The costs for the solar home systems are based on an insolation of 2000kWh/m². The battery capacity is 120Ah for the 120W panel and 75Ah for the 40W panel.
○ The load for the wind charger is 240kWh/year. The battery capacity is 120Ah.
○ The petrol generator set costs are calculated for a 3kVA system. The

(Continued over)

economic life is 7 years and the utilization factor is 10% and 5% respectively, which corresponds to an annual generation of 2628kWh and 1314kWh respectively. The petrol cost is US$0.70/L.

○ The cost of the distribution system is based on capital, operation and maintenance costs. Two values are used: low density (US$0.17/kWh) and high density (US$0.11/kWh) consumers.

○ The costs for hydro power are based on system capacity of 100kW, investment costs of US$1 million, economic lifetime 25 years and a utilization factor of 50%.

○ The diesel generator set costs are calculated for a 450kVA system. The economic lifetime is 7 years and the utilization factor of 25%.

○ The 600kW wind power farm is assumed to have 90% turbine availability and a utilization factor of 100%. The maintenance cost is US$3200/year.

○ The solar powered system (as part of a hybrid grid system) uses a 120W module and an insolation of 1500kWh/m^2. The annual energy generation is 180kWh per module. The cost of the mountings is not included.

○ Losses in inverters and distribution systems are not included in the calculations.

Source: Amelin 1998

intensive equipment such as micro-hydro).

Making the selection

Table 4.13 summarizes the information given in this chapter. It can be used to help with the initial selection of the most promising technologies. However, technical factors are not the only issues which need to be taken into account when making a decision. There are a number of social and financial issues which play a role. Chapter 7 contains a checklist on the social issues, with a particular emphasis on the gender aspects which need to be taken into account. Chapter 5 looks at the financial analysis of RPS.

Sizing and installing renewable energy technologies is a skilled job. The sizing is made more difficult because RPS are site specific and local data may not exist, only general data at the national level. However, the collection of data is expensive and takes time and expertise.

Therefore, a compromise often has to be found between the quality of data and the equipment selection. This is where expert help is needed. However, operating an RPS is not too difficult with some training and help for an initial period. Simple maintenance can be learnt, but major tasks require technical expertise.

System expansion can be expensive and it is always a good idea to see if any potential savings in energy consumption can be made.[3] Investment in improved energy efficiency is usually cheaper than investment in new generation sources and reduces utility bills.

[3] For ideas on how to do this see *Energy Efficiency for Small and Medium Enterprises* in the UNIFEM Energy and Environment Technology Source Books (IT Publications).

Table 4.13: Factors which influence the selection of a stand-alone electricity generating option

Option	Input	Reliability	Expertise	Costs	Advantages	Disadvantages
Diesel generator	Diesel oil	Reliable Needs maintenance on a regular basis	High and medium	Fuel is expensive	Generators easily available Spare parts available Expertise widely available	Batteries needed Noisy and smelly technology Uses fossil fuels
Micro-hydro	Falling water Fast-flowing rivers	Reliability is dependent on water flow	High, medium and low	High initial investment costs Low running costs	Fairly constant production, no batteries needed No large dams necessary No noise or pollution Little waste heat Simple and robust technology	Site specific Fixed size Needs year-round flows Advanced engineering needed
Wind energy	Constant and adequate wind	Reliable	High and medium	Initial cost is high	Well developed technology No hazardous by-products Easily coupled to diesel generator during periods of no wind	Technology needs batteries Limited to areas with steady wind Spare parts not always available
Solar PV	High levels of sunshine	Reliable	High, medium and low	Initial costs high Low running costs	Silent operation No pollution during use Sized to individual needs	Relatively small production Requires batteries Panels must be clean Panels are fragile

Option	Input	Reliability	Expertise	Costs	Advantages	Disadvantages
Gasifier	Wood chips, small branches, twigs, various agricultural residues (including rice husks, maize cobs, coconut) and waste paper	Depends on the resources size, moisture and ash content	High	Initial costs high Running costs depend on feedstock and source	Does not require batteries Production not dependent on weather circumstances	Regular maintenance and operation required Feedstock requirements demanding Needs diesel generator Problem of tar disposal Gas is poisonous in enclosed spaces
Biogas	Pig dung, cow dung, water, non-woody material, sheep dung and human waste	Reliable	High and medium	Initial investment costs are high	Effective use of dung provides manure and electricity Improves hygiene and sanitation	Collection of feedstock and water for feeding the plant can be time-consuming and add to women's burdens Size of digester is fixed so hard to match increases in demand Needs diesel generator
Steam	Wood straw, flax, bagasse coconut shells, rice husks, coal and peat	Reliable	High	High costs	Mature technology Uses waste	Small-scale systems not available Operation needs high skills

5
Financial aspects

Conducting a financial analysis

ONE OF THE main criteria of selection of a specific technology for electricity generation is the cost.[4] It is not always wise to choose the cheapest technology. Although the initial investment may be low, over the lifetime of the equipment the total costs might be significantly more than for a model with higher initial investment costs, due to, for example, more frequent repairs. When choosing an RPS there is frequently a trade-off between cost, performance and reliability.

Assessing the costs from the point of view of the user/beneficiary requires a systematic method of analysis, known as financial analysis, to allow comparison between the various options under consideration. The analysis indicates which RPS are financially feasible. Unfortunately, this analysis has to be carried out for each investment, since the costs are site specific.

In everyday English when looking at the costs and benefits of an investment the words 'financial' and 'economic' tend to be used interchangeably. However, for the economist they have very strict definitions. A *financial* analysis looks at the investment from the perspective of the end-beneficiary (e.g. farmer, cook, health centre). An *economic* analysis looks at the investment from the perspective of society as a whole. A full-scale economic analysis is not usually conducted for a household or micro-enterprise RPS but a community scheme might consider that this type of analysis would be needed to ensure that

there is effective use of scarce resources. However, at the household/micro-enterprise level, and certainly for initial calculations at the community level, a financial analysis is sufficient.

A financial analysis involves a number of steps, which are summarized as follows:

○ A detailed estimate is made of the necessary inputs (for example, money, equipment, land, labour) to the project, and the outputs expected from it.
○ A cash value is assigned to these inputs and outputs.
○ A cash flow (money expected to come in and be spent) on a year-by-year basis for the duration of the project is prepared.
○ A measure of profitability of the project is determined by systematically comparing the costs and benefits. A number of standard techniques, for example net present value, internal rate of return, benefit/cost ratio, have been developed for this – which have their own advantages and disadvantages. (See Resources for books where these techniques are explained.)
○ In making an estimate of costs and benefits, a number of assumptions are usually made – some of which are more valid than others; for example, the likely rate of interest at which the money can be borrowed. The effect

---

[4] Cost and price are sometimes used interchangeably by lay people. Economists are very strict in their definition of the two terms. *Cost* is the minimum amount that something (energy or an energy technology in our case) can be sold for to allow a reasonable return to the supplier. *Price* is the amount a purchaser is willing to pay for energy or an energy technology.

Table 5.1: Calculation of biogas plant payback period (in US$)

Year	0	1	2	3	4	5	6	7	8	9	10
Item											
Investment	−1100										
Annual returns		+200	+200	+200	+200	+200	+200	+200	+200	+200	+200
Debt remaining/ Accumulated savings	−1100	−900	−700	−500	−300	−100	+100	+300	+500	+700	+900

of using different values for the profitability of the project can be checked by using different figures.
○ The timing of loan repayments has to be checked to see if they will cause cash flow problems.

In the commercial context, valuing costs and benefits does not usually present problems, since they deal with traded commodities, such as raw materials and energy, which have identifiable prices. However, in the non-commercial context a number of problems can be encountered. For example, micro-hydro schemes using storage cookers to reduce time in firewood collection would include saving women and children's time as a benefit: but how to cost this? As a measure of the time saved in fuelwood collection one could assume, for example, that women would have more time to engage in income-generation activities and from that estimate the potential income. However, many women argue that they do not wish to be perceived in this way, other people argue that children should not be engaged in such activities. Many electrical appliances are valued because they are convenient to use – how do you value convenience in cash terms? There are no easy answers to this and at the project level it is probably best to keep the calculations as simple as possible. Remember that financial analysis is supposed to look at the project from the user's perspective and most users will never do such a calculation (do you make such a calculation when making a major purchase?). If people are going to purchase a technology they must be able to see the benefits of a technology for themselves. The main question will be 'How long will it take me to get back the money I have invested?'. Therefore, this is a method of financial analysis which reflects their perception of the situation.

A simple approach is the static payback period, which gives the potential user an idea of the risk she is undertaking. It does not make adjustments for inflation. It compares the payback period with the lifetime of the equipment. Most people in rural areas do not like to take out loans which will take more than a couple of harvests to repay. This will apply equally to households and micro-enterprises, since many of the latter are also closely linked to agricultural production. Table 5.1 shows a calculation for a biogas system using the static payback method. The column under Year 0 shows the initial investment costs. All the annual costs need to be estimated. Box 5.1 gives some indication of factors which have to be costed. (A similar list of factors could be

Box 5.1: Factors which require costing for the biogas system

Costs

Investment costs
○ Planning
○ Building digester and engine shed
○ Modification of animal housing
○ Diesel generator
○ Slurry spreading equipment
○ Assembly and commissioning
○ Taxes, duties, fees
○ Transportation

Time costs
○ Feeding the plant
○ Spreading the slurry
○ Acquiring and adding diesel fuel

Maintenance and repair
○ Spare parts/materials
○ Wages for maintenance/repair work

Benefits

Energy revenues
○ Market value of replaced energy
○ Energy sold to others
○ Increased production due to increased energy availability

Revenue from fertilizer
○ Market value of replaced fertilizer
○ Revenues from sale of digested slurry
○ Higher cash crop yields due to fertilizing with digested slurry

Time saved for additional
○ Income-generating work outside the farm
○ Work on the farm

devised for the other RPS systems.) These costs are then deducted from any income to give the annual returns. The annual returns are added to the investment expenditure every year to give the debt remaining (the third line in the table) until it either reaches zero or is positive. In this case the investment would be positive after 6 years, which is inside the lifetime of the digester (assumed to be at least 10 years). However, it is outside of the 3-year harvest guideline suggested above. Therefore, the woman considering the investment would then make similar calculations for other RPS to find a system with a shorter payback period or she could evaluate the other more difficult-to-quantify benefits of the biogas system (e.g. less nuisance from flies). A comparison should also be made with the energy costs of not investing in the RPS.

Access to credit

The initial cost of an RPS is a considerable barrier to gaining access to electricity. This situation is worse for women than men because their access to credit is more restricted. Commercial banks will require some form of collateral such as land or property, to which women frequently have no title. A husband or other male relative's signature can also be required. Therefore some attention needs to be given to how women can purchase RPS or raise the connection fee for grid electricity. There are an increasing number of financing organizations being set up which enable women's access to credit; the Grameen Bank in Bangladesh is probably the most well known. Women also organize their own informal savings clubs. Utilities should also be encouraged to provide loans.

6
Wiring and other safety aspects

INSTALLING ELECTRICAL SYSTEMS is a skilled task both for grid and for stand-alone systems and should be carried out by someone with appropriate training. If wiring a house or micro-enterprise is being done prior to connection to a grid, the utility (or other supplier) may make a number of stipulations: the work has to be carried out by an approved electrician. Houses and micro-enterprises which have been wired for grid electricity can use electricity from stand-alone systems, and likewise houses and micro-enterprises that have been wired for RPS can be connected up to the grid.

Household circuits

The inside of the house or micro-enterprise must be wired to be able to use the electricity. The electric current is distributed around the house and micro-enterprise via electric wire: copper wire covered with a plastic coating. Wiring comes in a range of sizes, usually sold on the basis of the cross-sectional area of the wire, for example, 1.0, 1.5, 2.5, 4.0, 6.0 and 10.0mm². 240V AC systems need a different type of wiring (1.0 or 1.5mm²) to low voltage DC systems (2.5mm²). A different size of wire will be needed for connecting the RPS to the battery. The type of wiring required should be discussed with the supplier before purchase.

It is important to take care of the plastic coating on the outside of the wire, since this prevents shocks. Not all plastic is resistant to decomposition resulting from prolonged exposure to sunlight.

Therefore wires coated in this type of plastic and those that are run underground or up outside walls should be run through a special type of plastic piping called conduit. This protects the cable against sunlight, as well as the risk of cutting through the cable with implements such as spades or being chewed by animals.

Electrical appliances come with a plug which is used to connect to the electricity supply by way of a socket (or power outlet) mounted on the wall. Plugs and sockets come in different shapes. The UK system, which is still used in many former Commonwealth countries, uses plugs with square pins (the part of the plug inserted into the socket) while the rest of the world uses round pins. However, these round pins can vary in thickness and distance apart. Electrical equipment is not always universally useable! Equipment that runs on DC usually comes supplied with a different type of plug to ensure that it is only connected to a DC supply, since connecting it to AC would damage it. DC sockets are not readily available and 240V AC sockets are sometimes used instead. Again this should be discussed with the supplier before making any purchase.

Switches are used to turn lamps, appliances and other equipment on and off. Sockets often come with an inbuilt switch and most appliances have switches.

An important component in an electrical circuit is a device which protects people against shocks and equipment against damage when faults, such as short-circuits, occur. There are two types of devices: fuses and miniature circuit breakers. Fuses are devices placed in the

Figure 6.1: Components of household wiring system

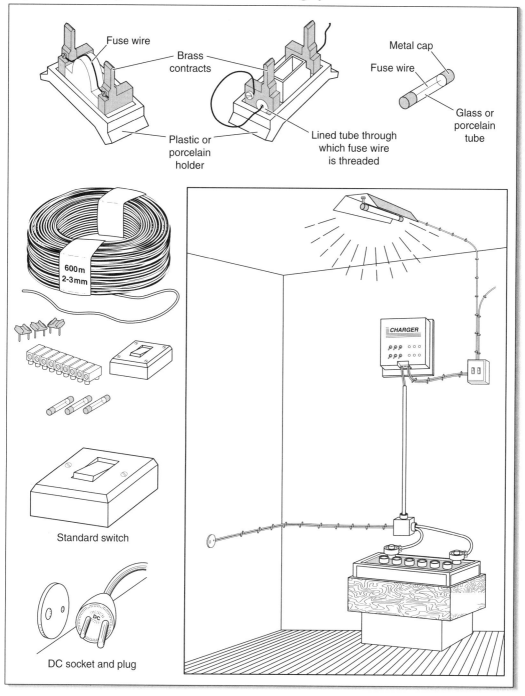

circuit which, when a short occurs, interrupt the supply of electricity. A fuse consists of a thin piece of wire which under normal operation allows the current to flow. However, if the current increases beyond safety levels, the fuse wire heats up quickly and melts (usually referred to as 'blows'). Once the problem causing the increased current has been repaired, the fuse needs to be replaced. (Square pin plugs from the British system also contain fuses which can blow. This enables the specific faulty piece of equipment to be disconnected from the supply rather than disconnecting the entire supply). Fuses vary in size and are rated in amps (0.25–30 amps would be the range for the applications in this book, although larger ones are possible). They are sized on the basis of the current they are protecting and should blow when the current exceeds the circuit's rated value by 20%.

An alternative to the fuse is the miniature circuit breaker. These are small switches which automatically switch off and break the circuit if there is a short-circuit. They can be switched on again once the problem has been repaired.

The order in which the appliances in the system are joined has practical implications. If the appliances are joined in series (wired up end to end in a continuous chain) and one of them fails, for example a lamp breaking, then the circuit is broken and none of the appliances will work until the broken lamp is replaced. The alternative method is to connect them in parallel, which means that the system is so connected that the 'removal' of one appliance in the system, for example a lamp breaking, would still allow the electric current to flow to the other appliances. This is the usual method for wiring households and micro-enterprises since it has the advantage that the rest of the system can function until repairs or replacements of the faulty component can be organized.

Safety aspects

There are dangers associated with using any energy conversion technology. Electricity is no exception. However, with proper attention to creating awareness in people not familiar with this form of energy on how to use it sensibly, electricity use is safe. Children and old people may need special consideration. There are two dangers associated with electricity: fire, which may break out if wiring is not properly installed, and electric shocks, which occur if there is physical contact with electric current. With proper care and expert installation and use, the risk of either of these occurring is very small. The risks are far smaller than those associated with fire from kerosene or candles and the health risks of smoke and carbon monoxide poisoning, which are associated with wood and charcoal fires.

The main structural way to avoid the dangers of electricity is to ensure that all wires, sockets and lighting outlets are properly insulated. All wiring should be covered with a plastic coating and all switches, plugs and sockets should be covered with plastic surfaces, so that it is not possible to see any of the metal wire. There should never be electric outlets close to water, near taps or in showers, etc. Trained electricians will be aware of all these things.

In some countries it is not permitted to connect temporary houses to the grid supply. By temporary is meant houses which are not securely built and in which there is risk of rainwater leaking in and coming into contact with electric wiring. Battery electricity (as used in combination with solar and wind generation systems for individual households) is generally low voltage and so is not dangerous (though sometimes an unpleasant tingling sensation will be felt).

It is particularly important that women and children who are not used to dealing with electricity are made familiar with a few simple safety rules that should ensure safe operation:

○ Never touch an electric wire if the outer covering is broken and the metal wire is exposed – get an appropriately qualified person to replace it;
○ Never touch plugs or switches with wet hands. Water and electricity should never be in direct contact because water is a good transmitter of electricity;
○ Treat the cables of electrical appliances with care, so that their outer covering does not fray and the wires in the plugs do not become loose. If they become frayed, have them fixed or replaced;
○ Do not stretch cables or leave them trailing across the floor where people walk. If a piece of electrical equipment should catch fire while switched on, first switch off the power at the main switch, before attempting to put out the fire. Never throw water on an electric fire;
○ Do not allow children to handle electric equipment unsupervised;
○ Never insert fingers or other objects into sockets.

Although books on the subject of electricity and utilities always recommend, and with good reason, using a certified electrician to carry out work involving installing electric circuits, people still do make connections themselves. These are often dangerous with exposed, bare wires. It would therefore be better to face up to this unpleasant fact and try to minimize the risk. Providing training to ensure that women are able to carry out simple, household wiring tasks themselves could do much to improve safety.

7
Facilitating women's access to stand-alone electricity generating systems

THE SELECTION OF an appropriate stand-alone technology for remote power generation depends on a number of technical and non-technical factors. The following checklists suggest some of the issues which need to be covered when assessing a particular situation (household, micro-enterprise or community) for the use of electricity and the gender aspects which need to be specifically taken into account.

Sizing the demand

○ Who needs the energy? (For communities this has to be broken down into different socio-economic groups. Are women's specific needs addressed?)
○ What is the energy needed for? Is electricity the most appropriate energy form for these applications?
○ How much energy is required on a daily basis? Are there seasonal fluctuations?
○ Are people aware of the different uses of electricity? (Men's and women's perceptions may differ.)
○ How much are they prepared to pay? Can they prioritize uses? Are these priorities the same for men and women? Who is making the decisions and about what (How much electricity? When? What generating form? Where will the supply be available? Sockets or light fittings?). Are women's needs in their reproductive, productive and community roles being addressed?

Assessing the technology

Table 4.13 presents an overview of the technical factors which influence the selection of the energy source for running the stand-alone systems described in Chapter 4. Specific questions which need to be asked about the different options include:

○ Is the resource available in sufficient quantities to match the demand when it is needed? How flexible is the technology to variations in demand?
○ Will batteries be capable of covering supply deficiencies at reasonable cost? Will other types of fallback technologies be required to ensure some level of energy service is always available?
○ How flexible is the technology as regards meeting future growth in demand?
○ What is the status of the technology, as regards local technical expertise? Are skills available nearby to install, maintain and repair the technology? Are spare parts readily available? Is the equipment imported or locally made?
○ What skills are required to install, maintain and repair the technology? Can women easily acquire these skills?
○ What is the cost of installation? Running costs?
○ What kind of guarantees does the supplier offer?
○ Does the conversion technology have more than one function? (For example,

biogas systems produce a fertilizer as well as gas for generating electricity, steam engines can produce process heat.) Who would benefit from these extra functions? Does this influence the selection of the technology?

o Are the system components for wiring a house and using electricity safely easily available? (Switches, insulated wire, fuses, etc?)

o Is appropriate electrical end-use equipment available? Does it require AC or DC?

o What skills are needed to operate the equipment?

o Does the supplier provide training on the use of the conversion technology and the use of electricity? On site or must the user travel to another location? Does this have any implications for women's access to electricity?

o How convenient is the RPS to use?

o Will the use of a particular technology increase women's burden?

o How safe is the RPS to use? Are there any health risks involved? Are these different for men and women?

o Are there cultural objections to women operating a particular technology?

o What are the environmental costs and benefits of the technology? Does the technology have different environmental impacts on men and women?

Assessing the community

o Are women consulted as to their preferences for particular electricity generating technologies? Are they able to make informed decisions?

o Will women have equal access to and control over the electricity if they wish to establish their own businesses?

o Will women have equal access to the technical training involved in the in-

stallation, operation and maintenance of the system? Will this training be tailored to women's particular needs?

o How will electrification influence women's activities and workloads?

o What kind of institutions will be needed for local management and will they function effectively? Do local management structures already involve women? How effectively?

Financial institutions

o How familiar are financial institutions with the different technological options?

o Are they prepared to lend for RPS?

o What type of collateral do they require on loans? Do they take into account the gender differences in access to collateral?

o Are they prepared to lend money for purchasing systems for household use? To energy entrepreneurs? Do they have different policies for men and women?

Giving women the confidence to use electricity and to participate in its generation

The arrival of electricity in a rural community is an exciting moment which opens up a range of new possibilities. People may not be familiar with electricity and they need some instruction in how to use it wisely and safely. They may have uncertainties which they will need help to overcome; for example, does the electricity seep out of the socket if there is no plug inserted in it? Likewise, for RPS they will need to acquire a number of new skills and learn how to deal with a new set of responsibilities. This then creates a need for training. However, it is important that the provision of any training takes gender issues into account. It is generally assumed that the generation of electricity, since it involves technology, must be of interest to men, and consequently men receive the training. There is no inherent reason why men should be interested in technology and indeed many men are not, nor may they have any wish to become involved. The parallel conception is that women are not interested, nor should they be interested, in energy technologies. Consequently, women can be excluded from training and so are denied opportunities to benefit from increasing skills through which they can become more responsible for meeting their own needs. Therefore, training in the generation and use of electricity should be made equally available to both men and women.

However, it is not sufficient to provide gender balance in access to training to ensure that women will benefit. The type and form of training is also important to ensure that women are able to maximize their opportunities. Unfortunately, at present most of the technical issues are dealt with by men in companies and NGOs. This means that the training will probably be given by men. If the training is not dealt with in a gender-sensitive way, it can undermine women's confidence. In some rural areas there may be cultural objections to women being trained by men. The training may be held at a distant location requiring staying away from home, which may conflict with women's domestic and childcare tasks. These factors need to be taken into account when designing the training so that they do not become a barrier to women's access to electricity. Where possible, mixed teams of trainers should be used and training should be as close to the women's homes as possible. Some other issues that need to be considered when assessing any training include:

○ Are the trainers gender sensitive?
○ Have the trainers experience of dealing with mixed groups, so that women are not marginalized and have their confidence undermined?
○ Is the training organized in such a way as to fit into both men's and women's availability and to reflect their different tasks and obligations?
○ Is the language and methodology used appropriate for women?

Becoming an energy entrepreneur

There are increasing possibilities for independent producers of electricity to sell to the utility grid or to become operators of mini-grids. Alternatively they can sell or lease stand-alone systems or they can provide a battery-charging service based on RPS. For women in rural areas, this provides an exciting opportunity to provide their community with an energy service, to have an income source and still be within easy reach of their households. However, to become entrepreneurs women often need a helping hand in translating a good idea into a realizable project. Training courses can be offered in how to become an energy entrepreneur.

The course should cover both technical training and business skills. Topics might include:

○ The overall structure and appropriate applications of typical small-scale renewable energy electricity generating systems.
○ General operating principles of typical system components.
○ How to obtain renewable energy site data (in-country sources or methods of estimation).

Case study: Vietnam Women's Union promotes PV systems in remote areas
The Vietnam Women's Union (VWU) Rural Electrification Project demonstrates how photovoltaic systems can hasten sustainable development in remote rural communities. With the support of the Solar Electric Light Fund, the Rockefeller Brothers Fund and Sandia National Laboratories, the VWU installed photovoltaic lighting systems in 130 households and five community centres, as well as photovoltaic-powered street lights in two Vietnamese village markets. These energy systems have helped to stimulate business and educational opportunities in the Mekong River Delta and in Northern Vietnam.

Around 85% of the Vietnamese people live without electricity and the chances of connection to the public grid are slim. They now use kerosene lamps with the corresponding health and safety problems. VWU has about 11 million members and together with SELF they started a joint solar project. Its ultimate goal is to assemble and sell household solar systems using consumer financing provided by revolving credit managed by the VWU.

For this first pilot project, 14 local technicians were trained. As the bamboo houses in Vietnam are rebuilt every few years, the standard support frame for the solar panel was altered for mounting on a pole beside the house rather than incorporating the panel into the roof.

Despite minor installation problems, the SELF-VWU project has been successful and has caused excitement among rural community members. The PV-systems have provided light for using sewing machines after dark, contributing to an increase in small-scale garment production. The street lights installed in the market places, provide an element of safety that has extended trading hours. The community systems provide entertainment and education with colour televisions and video.

Individual Vietnamese families financed their own photovoltaic systems through the revolving fund established by SELF and managed by VWU. The revolving credit system has been highly successful. Ninety-five per cent of the payments are made on time and there has been no problem with defaults.

One negative aspect of using photovoltaic systems is old battery disposal. To alleviate this problem, SELF plans to implement a deposit-refund recycling programme. Old batteries will be returned for a discount on replacement and then be repaired for reuse.

Source: SELF/Caddet Technical brochure No. 28

○ How to size and design an RPS.
○ Installing and commissioning an RPS.
○ Operating and maintaining a mini-grid or stand-alone system.
○ Electrical wiring systems, regulations and safety.
○ Sources of information on equipment suppliers.

○ How to set up and manage a business.
○ How to conduct a market survey and interpret the results.
○ How to write a business plan and raise the finance.
○ How to negotiate with the utility.

Women need to increase their confidence with equipment. Therefore, the training schedule should have a significant amount of time allocated to practical skills acquisition, giving plenty of opportunity for hands-on experience. Women whose intention is to hire (male) expertise to carry out the day-to-day work should also be encouraged to participate, since this will increase their control over their business. Site visits should also be included, particularly to meet other women entrepreneurs (even if they are not involved in energy services, they can still serve as good role models). It would be particularly useful to include sessions on dealing with prejudice, since women will probably encounter resistance from male entrepreneurs, suppliers and potential clients who consider that this is not 'appropriate work for women'.

Resources

Bibliography

General

Energia News: the newsletter of the Network for Women and Sustainable Energy, contains case studies and articles about women and electricity.
Contact Energia at ETC, PO Box 64, 3830 AB Leusden, The Netherlands (e-mail:energia@ectnl.nl).
Financing Renewable Energy Projects: A guide for development workers, J. Gregory et al., ITP, London. ISBN 1–85339–387–8.
Fuelling Development – Energies for developing countries, Congress of the United States Office of Technology Assessment, 1992. OTA-E-516, Washington DC. US Government Printing Office. ISBN 0–16–036185–0.
Independent Energy Guide: Electrical power for home, boat and RV, K Jeffrey, Chelsea Green Publishing, 1995. ISBN 0–9644112–0–2.
The Power Guide: An international catalogue of small-scale energy equipment, W. Hulscher and P. Fraenkel, IT Publications Ltd, London, 1994. ISBN 1-85339-192-1.
RAPS Manual, University of Cape Town Energy for Rural Development Research Centre, 1992. ISBN 0–7992–1435–3.
Renewable Energy Assessments: An energy planner's manual, M.M. Gowan, East-West Centre, Hawaii, 1985.
Rural Energy Services, T. Anderson et al., ITP London, 1999. ISBN 1–85339–462–9.
Small-Scale Renewable Energy Sources for Rural Electrification: Possibilities and limitations, M. Amelin, 1998, Department of Electrical Power Engineering, Royal Institute of Technology, Stockholm, Sweden and Swedish International Development Co-operation Agency (SIDA).

Solar

Solar Electric Systems for Africa, M. Hankins, Commonwealth Science Council (UK) and AGROTEC (Harare, Zimbabwe), 1995.
Solar Photovoltaic Products: A guide for development workers, A. Derrick et al., IT Publications, London, 1991. ISBN 1–85339–002–X.
Solar Electricity, S. Roberts, Prentice Hall, 1991. ISBN 0–13825–068–5.

Biogas

Running a Biogas Programme: A handbook, D. Fulford, IT Publications, London, 1988. ISBN 0–94668–849–4.
Engines for Biogas: Theory, modification, economic operation, K. Von Mitzlaff, GATE, Germany, 1988.

Steam

Wood as an Energy Resource, D.A. Tillman, Academic Press, 1984.

Diesel Engine

Diesel and Gas Turbine Catalog: Worldwide engine power products directory and buyers guide, Diesel and Gas Turbine Publications, Wisconsin, USA.
Available from 13555 Bishop's Court, Brookfield, WI 53005–6286, USA. Phone: +1 414 784 9177: Fax: +1 414 784 8311.
Getting the Most from your Diesel Engine, C. Grauw, Botswana Technology Centre, Gaborone, 1987.
Available from Botswana Technology Centre, P/Bag 0082, Gaborone, Botswana.

Micro-Hydro

Micro-Hydro Power: A guide for development workers, P. Fraenkel et al., IT Publications, London, 1991. ISBN 1–85339–029–1.
Micro-Hydro Design Manual: A guide to small-scale water power schemes, A. Harvey et al., IT Publications, London, 1993. ISBN 1–85339–103–4.
Micro-hydro Electric Power, R.E. Holland, IT Publications, London, 1983.
Micro-hydropower Sourcebook, A.R. Inversin, NRECA, Washington DC, 1986. ISBN 0–94668–848–6.
MHP Information Package: A selected, annotated and classified bibliography on Micro Hydropower Development, U. Meier and A. Arter, SKAT, Switzerland, and GATE, Germany.

Wind

Introduction to Wind Energy, E.H. Lysen, CWD publication, May 1983, TOOL.
A Guide to Small Wind Energy Conversion Systems. J.Twidell (ed), Cambridge University Press, 1987.
It's a Breeze! A Guide to Choosing Windpower, H. Piggott, Centre for Alternative Technology, 1998. ISBN 1–898049 19X.

Internet sites

It is impossible to give a complete list of relevant Internet sites. However, a number of the most useful are given in this and the following section. Each site usually contains links to other sites.

ENERGIA
www.ENERGIA.org

American Wind Energy Association
www.awea.org

British Wind Energy Association
www.bwea.com

Lister-Petter Diesels
www.lister-petter.co.uk

Women and New and Renewable Source of Energy
solstice.crest.org/renewables/women-and-energy/index.html

CREST
solstice.crest.org/renewables/

IIEC Sustainable Energy Guide
solstice.crest.org/efficiency/iiec-seguide/index.html

IT Power Ltd
www.itpower.co.uk

Lotus Energy
www.south-asia.com/Nepaliug/lotus/

National Rural Electric Cooperative Association (NRECA)
www.nreca.org/

Solar Electric Light Fund
www.self.org/

Winrock International Renewable Energy Division
www.winrock.org/what/energy.asp/

Sensible Steam Consultants
www.sensiblesteam.com

World Wide Info System for Renewable Energy (WIRE)
www.wire1.ises.org/

Useful organizations

AIT (Asian Institute of Technology)
PO Box 4
Klong Luang
Pathumthani 12120
Bangkok
Thailand
Tel: +66 2 516 0110
Fax: +66 2 516 2126
www.ait.ac.th

APACE
C/o University of Technology
PO Box 123
Broadway, NSW 2007
Australia
Tel: +61 2 9514 2554
Fax: +61 2 9514 2611
www.apace.org.au

CAMARTEC
Biogas Extension Service
PO Box 764
Arusha
Tanzania
Tel: 255 57 8250
Fax: 225 57 8250

CAT (Centre for Alternative Technology)
Machynlleth
Powys
Wales SY20 9AZ
United Kingdom
Tel: +44 1654 702400
Fax: +44 1654 702782
www.cat.org.uk

CRES (Centre Régionale d'Energie Solaire)
BP 1872
Bamako
Mali

EDRC (Energy & Development Research Centre)
University of Cape Town
Private Bag
Rondebosch 770
South Africa
Tel: +27 21 650 2830
Fax: +27 21 650 3230
www.edrc.uct.ac.za

ENDA
4&5 Rue Kleber
BP 3370
Dakar
Senegal
Tel: +221 8 22 42 29/21 60 27
Fax: +221 8 22 26 95
www.enda.sn

FAKT/Hydronet
Stephan-Blattman Strasse 11
7743 Furtwangen
Germany
Tel: +49 7723 4459
Fax: +49 7723 5373

FWD (Foundation for Woodstove Dissemination)/AFREPREN
PO Box 30979
Nairobi
Kenya
Tel: 254 2 566032
Fax: 254 2 561464

GATE
Dag-Hammarskjold Weg 1
PO Box 5180
D-65726 Eschborn 1
Germany
Tel: +49 6 196 79 3185
Fax: +49 6 196 79 7352
www.gate.gtz.de

GTZ (German Agency for Technical Co-operation)
Dag-Hammarskjold Weg 1
PO Box 5180
D-65760 Eschborn 1
Germany
Tel: +49 61 96 79 0
Fax: +49 61 96 79 1115
www.gtz.de

Hangzhou International Centre on Small Hydro Power
136 Nanshan Road
PO Box 202
310002 Hangzhou
China
Tel: +86 571 70 70070
Fax: +86 571 70 23353
www.digiserve.com/inshp

INFORSE
Blegdamsvej 4 B, 1
DK-2200 Copenhagen N
Denmark
Tel: +45 3524 7700
Fax: +45 3524 7717
www. inforse.org

Intermediate Technology Development Group
Schumacher Centre
Bourton Hall
Bourton on Dunsmore
Rugby CV23 9QV
United Kingdom
Tel: +44 1788 661100
Fax: +44 1788 661101
www.oneworld.org/itdg

ISES (International Solar Energy Society)
International Headquarters
Villa Tannheim
Wiesentalstr 50
D-79115 Freiburg I Br
Germany
Tel: +49 761 45906 0
Fax: +49 761 45906 99
www.ises.org

KENGO (Kenyan Energy Non-Governmental Organizations Association)
PO Box 48917
Mwanzi Road
Westlands
Nairobi
Kenya
Tel: +254 2 749747/748281
Fax: +254 2 749382

Lund Centre for Habitat Studies
Lund University
Box 118
S-221 LUND
Sweden
Tel: +46 46 222 0000
Fax: +46 46 222 0800
www.ark3.lth.se

Natural Resources Institute
Central Avenue
Chatham Maritime
Kent ME4 4TB
United Kingdom
Tel: +44 1634 880088
Fax: +44 1634 880066/77
www.nri.org

RERIC
AIT
GPO Box 2754
Bangkok 10501
Thailand
Tel: +66 2 624 5863
Fax: +66 2 524 5870
www.ait.ac.th/clair/centers/reric

SEI (Stockholm Environment Institute)
Box 2142
S-10314 Stockholm
Sweden
Tel: +46 8412 1400
Fax: +46 8723 0348
www.sei.se

SKAT
Swiss Centre for Appropriate Technology
Vadianstrasse 42
CH-9000 St. Gallen
Switzerland
Tel: +41 71 228 5454
Fax: +41 71 228 5455
www.skat.ch

SOPAC
Energy Unit
Private Mail Bag
GPO
Suva, Fiji Islands
Tel: +679 381 377
Fax: +679 370 040
www.sopac.org

SPIRE (South Pacific Institute for Renewable Energy Research)
PO Box 11530
Mahina
Tahiti

Technology and Development Group (TDG)
University of Twente
PO Box 217
7500 AE Enschede
The Netherlands
Tel: +31 53 4893545
Fax: +31 53 4893081
www.utwente.nl/tdg

TERI (Tata Energy Research Institute)
Dabari Seth Block
Habitat Place
Lodhi Road
New Delhi 110003
India
Tel: +91 11 462 2246/460 1550
Fax: +91 11 462 1770/463 2609
www.teriin.org

TCC (Technology Consultancy Center)
University of Science and Technology
Kumasi
Ghana
Tel: +233 51 60323
Fax: +233 51 60232/3173

Appendices

Appendix 1: Electricity basics

Electricity is a form of energy (*electrical energy*). It is caused by the flow of electrons (minute particles or packets of energy) through a conducting medium. Electricity is invisible, which can make it difficult for people to understand how it works. However, there is a lot of similarity in the behaviour of electricity and water. We can see water, which means we are all familiar with the way it behaves! Therefore, a good understanding of electricity can be gained from considering an analogy with water. Figure A.1 shows a bucket filled with water. A small cup can be filled with water by opening a tap, inserted in the side near the bottom of the bucket.

Figure A.1: Bucket with tap

When the tap is opened water flows out through the pipe. Scientists say that this happens because the water in the bucket creates a pressure which, as soon as the tap opens, forces the water through the tap. The more water in the bucket, the greater the pressure or force of water.

When the tap is closed the water stays in the bucket, even though there is pressure for it to try to escape. Scientists describe this as the tap creating a resistance to flow. Opening the tap reduces the resistance to flow and the water is able to escape.

If the tap is left open, the water will flow out until there is no more water and the bucket is empty. How long this takes will depend upon two factors: how much water is present and by how much the tap isopened. The more open the tap (that is the lower the resistance), the quicker the water leaves and the sooner the bucket is empty. The more water in the bucket, the longer it takes to completely empty the bucket for a given amount of tap opening.

Another observation about water is that it does not flow uphill! Water always flows from a higher point to a lower point. Water in a lake or dam in the mountains can be released to flow downhill and when it does it can be used to turn a water mill or wheel lower down the mountain or hill. Scientists describe the water stored in the dam or lake as an energy store (*potential energy*), and the difference in height between the water and the water mill as a *potential difference*. (The water in the bucket also has potential energy relative to the cup.) The potential energy of the water in the dam is converted into mechanical energy when the water flows downhill and turns the waterwheel. The amount of potential energy depends upon the relative

(Continued over)

positions of the water and the mill. The greater the vertical distance between the two (or the more water in the dam), the larger the potential difference, and hence a larger amount of stored energy. Potential energy has different forms, for example, a battery, which has potential energy stored in the chemicals. Potential energy can be converted into different types of energy (for example, the chemical energy in a battery can be converted into electrical energy).

These ideas of energy flow and storage can now be used to describe how electricity works. The bucket is replaced by a source of electricity, for example a battery, the cup is replaced by a light bulb, and joining the two is a wire with a switch (equivalent to the pipe and tap respectively). (Figure 2.1) There is a potential difference between the battery and the light bulb. Therefore by opening the switch (the on-position), energy can flow along the wire from the source of higher potential energy (battery) to the part of the circuit with the lower potential energy. Electricity does not flow from the light bulb to the battery, just as water does not flow uphill. The source of electricity, the wire, switch and end-use form a circuit. Electricity flowing through a circuit is known as an *electric current*.

When the switch in the circuit is closed (the off-position) it provides a resistance to the flow of the electricity. If the switch is left in the on-position, electricity will continue to flow from the battery to the light bulb until there is no more electricity left in the battery and the battery is empty (sometimes referred to as a *flat* battery).

The wire in the circuit is equivalent to the pipe from the bucket, it channels the water to where it is needed. The wire is made of metal, usually copper. Materials through which electrons can move freely are called *conductors*. Metals and water are good conductors. However, not all materials are good conductors. Poor conductors, such as wood, plastic and rubber, are known as *insulators*. To ensure that electricity does not seep away from the conducting wire, it is coated with a layer of insulating plastic. Appendix 2 has some more information on conductors and resistors.

Returning to our water analogy, it was pointed out above that water does not flow uphill. However, it does flow backwards and forwards at regular intervals, under the influence of tides. The same holds for an electric current. The current can flow in one direction only, when it is known as *direct current* (DC), or in opposite directions, the direction of flow changing at regular, frequent intervals, which is known as *alternating current* (AC). DC is the type of current produced by batteries and power stations. AC is the form of electric current delivered to households. (See Box 2.3 for further explanation).

Appendix 2: Conductors and resistors

The quantity of electricity flowing through a wire depends upon two factors: the voltage (driving force) and the resistance (symbol R, unit ohm Ω) of the material through which the current flows. The relationship between these three factors is expressed by *Ohm's Law*:

voltage (V) = current (I) × resistance (R).

This relationship can be used in a number of ways. It tells us that if the resistance is high, then a high voltage is needed to overcome the resistance to enable the current to flow. (This can be compared to the force used to push a stationary object, for example, a car that has stalled.) Alternatively, the amount of current flowing in a circuit for a given voltage will depend upon the resistance of the material in the circuit. Some materials have a low resistance and are called conductors, for example, copper. These materials are used to transport (or conduct) electricity. Other materials have a high resistance, such as glass and ceramics, and are used as insulators. The amount of resistance depends upon the materials the circuit components are made of, the distance the electricity has to travel through a particular component, the cross-section of the individual component, and the temperature.

The resistance of the wire or appliance impedes the flow of current and converts the electrical energy to heat. The conversion of electricity to heat can be viewed as useful in an electric kettle or space heater or as a loss of energy when transmitting electricity a long a wire from a generator to the point of use of the electricity. There will always be some loss of energy when transmitting electricity, and utilities adopt a number of strategies to reduce these losses to a minimum. It is therefore a good idea to always site an RPS as close to the point of electricity use as is feasible and safe. Equipment suppliers should give advice on suitable distances.

Appendix 3: Important points for entrepreneurs using induction motors

In an AC circuit, inductance and capacitance loads can add to resistance loads. They 'consume' the input power without contributing to the useful output energy and are known as 'reactive loads'. In practical situations these reactive loads occur in rotating machinery such as generators and motors.

The input power and the output power for a rotating machine are linked by the 'power factor' defined as:

Power factor=P_m/VI where P_m is the mean or useful power and V and I are the voltage and current in the circuit.

The power factor can also be expressed as useful power (in kW) divided by apparent power (in kVA). In most situations a customer is charged for kVA consumption since this is what the supplier has delivered rather than the kW which the customer is making use of. It is relatively easy to improve a low power factor, and a customer who suspects that her power factor is low, for example, loads dominated by motors, is advised to seek professional advice, from electricity supplier or an appropriate expert to improve the situation.

Micro-enterprise owners who are considering using induction motors also need to analyse what form of AC supply they will be able to receive: *single phase* or *3-phase*. Utilities supply households with a form of AC current known as single phase. In-dustrial users also receive this type of supply and if they are using induction mo-tors, for technical reasons, they can be offered a second supply of *three-phase* from which to run this type of equipment. Single phase offers less complicated wiring, insulation arrangements and switches than three phase. If the micro-enterprise needs both types of supply it is necessary to install two wiring circuits. Entrepreneurs are strongly urged to discuss their requirements with an appropri-ately qualified professional.

Appendix 4: Important relationships involving current and voltage

Power = Voltage × Current   which can be written in shorthand as $P = V \times I$
This relationship can be used to calculate the current that is needed to run a certain appliance. For example, a 60W light bulb in a 220V electric system needs 0.27A:

$$60W = 220V \times I \qquad I = 60/220 = 0.27A$$

The capacity of batteries is often expressed in amp-hours (Ah). From this value it can be calculated for how many hours the battery will power a specific set of equipment. For example, a 30W radio is left on for 6 hours every day, and is powered by a 100Ah battery. Batteries have a much lower voltage than mains electricity. Car batteries and dry batteries are usually 12V. Therefore, the radio requires a current of 30/12 = 2.5A and the number of amp hours per day = 2.5 × 6 = 15Ah
The battery would therefore provide electricity for around 6 days without recharging – as long as the radio was the only equipment operating in the circuit! The more equipment in the circuit the shorter the time before the battery is flat (that is, needs recharging).

Acronyms

CIDA	Canadian International Development Assistance
NGO	Non-Governmental Organization
RPS	Remote Power System(s)
A	amp
Ah	ampere-hour
Hz	Hertz (cycles per second)
I	current
J	joule
kJ	kilojoule
kW	kilowatt
kWh	kilowatt-hour
MJ	megajoule
Ni–Cad	nickel-cadmium
MW	megawatt
Ω	ohms
Wp or Wp	peak watts
P	power
R	resistance
kVA	apparent power (kilovoltamperes)
V	volt/voltage
W	watt
Wh	watt-hour
W_{el}	Watts electric